INSTRUCTOR'S MANUAL

FUTURES, OPTIONS AND SWAPS
SECOND EDITION

Robert W. Kolb

ISBN: 1-57718-085-2

BLACKWELL
Publishers
Malden, MA & Oxford, UK

Printed in the United States of America

99 98 97 96 -- 9 8 7 6 5 4 3 2

ISBN: 1-57718-085-2

Contents

1
Introduction

Answers to Questions and Problems

1. If an arbitrage opportunity did exist in a market, how would traders react? Would the arbitrage opportunity persist? If not, what factors would cause the arbitrage opportunity to disappear?

    Traders are motivated by profit opportunities, and an arbitrage opportunity represents the chance for riskless profit without investment. Therefore, traders would react to an arbitrage opportunity by trading to exploit the opportunity. They would buy the relatively underpriced asset and sell the relatively overpriced asset. The arbitrage opportunity would disappear, because the presence of the arbitrage opportunity would create excess demand for the underpriced asset and excess supply of the overpriced asset. The arbitrageurs would continue their trading until the arbitrage opportunity disappeared.

2. Explain why it is reasonable to think that prices in a financial market will generally be free of arbitrage opportunities.

    Generally arbitrage opportunities will not be available in financial markets because well-informed and intelligent traders are constantly on the lookout for such chances. As soon as an arbitrage opportunity appears, traders trade to take advantage of the opportunity, causing the mispricing to be corrected.

3. Explain the difference between a derivative instrument and a financial derivative.

    A derivative is a financial instrument or security whose payoffs depend on any underlying asset. A financial derivative is a financial instrument or security whose payoffs depend on an underlying financial instrument or security.

4. What is the essential feature of a forward contract that makes a futures contract a type of forward contract?

A forward contract always involves the contracting at one moment in time with the performance under the contract taking place at a later date. Thus, futures represent a kind of forward contract under this definition.

5. Explain why the purchaser of an option has rights and the seller of an option has obligations.

The purchaser of an option makes a payment which is the consideration given to acquire certain rights. By contrast, the seller of an option receives payment at the time of sale and undertakes certain obligations in return for that payment.

6. In a futures contract, explain the right and obligations of the buyer or seller. How does this compare with an option contract?

In a futures contract, both the buyer and the seller have both obligations and rights. The buyer of a futures contract promises to make payment and take delivery at a future date, while the seller of a futures contract promises to make delivery and receive payment at a future date. This contrasts with the option market in which the buyer has only rights and the seller has only obligations following the original transaction.

7. Explain the difference between an option on a physical good and an option on a futures.

An option on a physical good gives the owner the right to buy the physical good by paying the exercise price and the seller of an option is obligated to deliver the good. When the owner of either a call or put futures option exercises, no delivery of any physical good occurs. Instead, both the buyer and seller of the futures option receive a position in a futures contract.

8. What is the essential feature of a swap agreement?

Essentially, a swap agreement obligates the two counterparties to make payments to each other over time. These payment streams can be tied to the value of interest rate sensitive instruments, to foreign currency values, to the fluctuating value of physical commodities, or to any other item of value.

9. Distinguish between interest rate swaps and currency swaps.

   In an interest rate swap, one party pays to another a fixed rate of interest, while the second party pays a floating rate of interest. Generally, no principal changes hands, but the promised payments are tied to some measure of interest rates. In a currency swap, payments between the two counterparties are typically made in different currencies and there is often an initial exchange of principal amounts in different currencies at the outset of the swap agreement.

10. What is a complete market? Can you give an example of a truly complete market? Explain.

    A **complete market** is a market in which any and all identifiable payoffs can be obtained by trading the securities available in the market. A complete market is essentially a theoretical ideal and is unlikely to be observed in practice.

11. Explain how the existence of financial derivatives enhances speculative opportunities for traders in our financial system.

    Speculators can use financial derivatives to profit from their correct anticipation of changes in interest rates, currency values, stock market levels, and so on. Financial derivatives are particularly powerful speculative instruments because they can be managed to give specific risk exposures while avoiding risks that are unwanted. In addition, financial derivatives markets are often more liquid than the underlying markets and financial derivatives can be traded with lower transaction costs in many instances.

12. If financial derivatives are as risky as their reputation indicates, explain in general terms how they might be used to reduce a pre–existing risk position for a firm.

    While an outright position in a financial derivative considered in isolation generally embodies considerable risk, these instruments can be used to offset other pre–existing risks that a firm might face. For example, a savings and loan association might face potential losses due to rising interest rates and this risk might arise from the normal conduct of its business. Such an association could use interest rate futures, options on interest rate futures, or swap agreements to offset that pre–existing risk. Properly managed, financial derivatives can reduce a pre–existing business risk through hedging.

2
Futures Markets

Answers to Questions and Problems

1. Explain the different roles of a floor broker and an account executive.

    A floor broker is located on the floor of the exchange and executes orders for traders off the floor of the exchange. Typically, the floor broker will either be an independent trader who executes orders on a contractual basis for a futures commission merchant (FCM), or the floor broker may be an employee of an FCM. An account executive is almost always employed by an FCM and is located off the floor of the exchange. The account executive is the person one typically thinks of as a broker. The account executive could be located in the local office of any major brokerage firm and has customers for whom he or she executes orders by communicating them to the exchange via the communication facilities of the FCM.

2. At a party, a man tells you that he is an introducing broker. He goes on to explain that his job is introducing prospective traders such as yourself to futures brokers. He also relates that he holds margin funds as a service to investors. What do you make of this explanation?

    The guy is a fraud. First, a defining characteristic of an introducing broker (IB) is that the IB does not hold customers' funds. Instead, the IB is associated with an FCM who holds the customers' funds. Second, the last person the IB wants his customer to meet is another broker. The IB's income depends on executing orders for his customers, so the IB wants to keep his flock of customers away from the wolves (other brokers) that are hungry for customers.

3. Assume that you are a floor broker and a friend of yours is a market maker who trades soybeans on the floor of the Chicago Board of Trade. Beans are trading at $6.53 per bushel. You receive an order to buy beans and you buy one contract from your friend at $6.54, one cent above the market. Who wins, who loses, and why? Explain the rationale for making such practice illegal.

    As described, this transaction costs your customer $.01 per bushel and transfers those funds to the friend from whom you purchase the contract at $6.54. On a 5,000 bushel contract, this amounts to $50. Thus, as described, the customer loses and the friend wins. It is important to see the motivation for the floor broker's engaging in this transaction. As described, the floor broker cheats her customer and helps the friend. Presumably, the motivation for such an action is the expectation that the friend will return the favor on another transaction. The rationale for making this transaction illegal is clear; it amounts to a direct theft from the customer.

4. Back at the party after several more hours. Your buddy from Question 2 buttonholes you again and starts to explain his great success as a dual trader, trading both beans and corn. What do you think?

   This guy is not bright. A dual trader is a person who trades for his or her own account and who executes orders for others at the same time.

5. You are having trouble escaping from your friend in Question 4. He goes on to explain that liquidation–only trading involves trading soybean against soyoil to profit from the liquidation that occurs when beans are crushed. Explain how your understanding of "liquidation–only trading" differs from your friend's.

   We hope that your understanding of liquidation–only trading runs as follows: Under liquidation–only trading each trade must result in a reduction of a trader's open interest. Every trade must be an offsetting trade. Liquidation–only trading essentially amounts to the closing of a market, and this is done during serious market disturbances, such as a manipulation. Liquidation–only trading has nothing in particular to do with beans or any other commodities.

6. In purchasing a house, contracting to buy the house occurs at one time. Typically, closing occurs weeks later. At the closing the buyer pays the seller for the house and the buyer takes possession. Explain how this transaction is like a futures or forward transaction.

   The purchase of a house has many features of a forward contract. Contracting occurs at one date, with performance on the contract occurring later at the closing. In buying a house, there is usually a good faith deposit or earnest money put up at the time of contracting. The contract is tailored to the individual circumstances, with the performance terms and the closing date being agreed on between the buyer and seller. The contract is not like a futures, because there is no organized exchange, the contract terms are not fixed, and settlement can occur at any time instead of at a fixed date.

7. In the futures market, a widget contract has a standard contract size of 5,000 widgets. What advantage does this have over the well–known forward market practice of negotiating the size of the transaction on a case–by–case basis? What disadvantages does the standardized contract size have?

   With standardized contract size and other terms, a futures contract avoids uncertainty about what is being traded. If these terms were not specified, traders would have to specify all of the features of the underlying good anew each time there is a contract. The futures style of trading has the disadvantage of losing flexibility due to the standardization. For example, the amount of the contract is fixed, as is the quality of the underlying good, and the time the contract will be settled.

8. What factors need to be considered in purchasing a commodity futures exchange seat? What are all the possible advantages that could come from owning a seat?

A seat on a commodity exchange is essentially a capital asset. The purchaser would want to consider the risk, including systematic risk, associated with such a purchase. The value of the seat depends mainly on the expected trading volume on the exchange, so we expect seat prices to be sensitive to the business cycle and to competition from foreign exchanges. Owning a seat allows one to trade on the exchange. Also, the seat holder can lease the seat for someone else to trade. Therefore, the seat offers the potential for cash inflows as well as capital appreciation.

9. Explain the difference between initial and maintenance margin.

Initial margin is the amount a trader must deposit before trading is permitted. Maintenance margin is the minimum amount that must be held in the trader's account while a futures position is open. If the account value falls below the amount specified as the maintenance margin, the trader must deposit additional funds to bring the account value back to the level of the initial margin.

10. Explain the difference between maintenance and variation margin.

Maintenance margin is the amount a trader must keep in the account to avoid a margin call. Variation margin is the payment a trader must make in a margin call. The margin call occurs when the account value drops below the level set for the maintenance margin. Upon receiving a margin call the trader must make a cash payment of the variation margin. The maintenance margin is a stock variable, while the variation margin is a flow variable.

11. On February 1, a trader is long the JUN wheat contract. On February 10, she sells a SEP wheat futures, and sells a JUN wheat contract on February 20. On February 15, what is her position in wheat futures? On February 25, what is her position? How would you characterize her transaction on February 20?

On February 15, the trader holds an intra–commodity spread, being long the JUN and short the SEP wheat. On February 25, the trader is short one SEP wheat contract. The transaction on February 20 was a transaction offsetting the original long position in SEP wheat.

12. Explain the difference between volume and open interest.

Open interest is the number of contracts currently obligated for delivery. The volume is the number of contracts traded during some period. For every purchase there is a sale, and the purchase and sale of one contract generates one contract of trading volume.

13. Define "tick" and "daily price limit."

A tick is the minimum amount a futures contract can change. For example, in the T–bond contract, the tick size is 1/32 of one point of par. This gives a dollar tick value of $31.25 per T–bond futures contract. The daily price limit is the amount the contract can change in price in one day. It is usually expressed as some number of ticks, and it is measured from the previous day's settlement price. No trade can be executed at a price that differs from the previous day's settlement price by more than the daily price limit.

14. A trader is long one SEP crude oil contract. On May 15, he contracts with a business associate to receive 1,000 barrels of oil in the spot market. The business associate is short one SEP crude oil contract. How can the two traders close their futures positions without actually transacting in the futures market?

The traders close their futures positions through an exchange for physicals transaction (EFP). In an EFP, two traders with futures positions exchange the physical good for cash and report this transaction to the exchange, asking the exchange to offset their futures contracts against each other. This transaction is also called an ex–pit or against actuals transaction.

15. Explain how a trader closes a futures market position via cash settlement.

For a contract satisfied by cash settlement, there is no delivery. Instead, when the futures contract expires, the final settlement price on the futures is set equal to the cash price for that date. This practice ensures convergence of the futures price and the cash price. Traders then make or receive payments based on the difference between the previous day's settlement price and the final settlement price on the contract.

16. Explain "price discovery."

In futures markets, price discovery refers to the revealing of information about future prices that the market facilitates. It is one of the two major social functions of the futures market. (The other is risk transference.) As an example, the futures price for wheat for delivery in nine months reveals information to the public about the expected future spot price of wheat at the time of delivery. While controversial, there is some reason to believe that the futures price (almost?) equals the spot price that is expected to hold at the futures expiration. This price discovery function helps economic agents plan their investment and consumption by providing information about future commodity prices.

17. Contrast anticipatory hedging with hedging in general.

In anticipatory hedging a trader enters the futures market and transacts before (or in anticipation of) some cash market transaction. This differs from a hedge of an existing position. For example, a farmer might sell wheat futures in anticipation of the harvest. Alternatively, a merchant holding an inventory of wheat might hedge the inventory by selling wheat futures. The farmer is engaged in anticipatory hedging, because he or she is expecting to have the cash market position and hedges this anticipation. The wheat merchant already has the cash market position, in virtue of holding the wheat inventory, and therefore is not engaged in anticipatory hedging.

18. What is "front running"?

Front running is a market practice in which a broker holds a customer's order for execution and executes a similar order of his or her own before executing the customer's order. This practice can be particularly pernicious if the customer's order is large, because the order may itself move prices. By front running, the broker seeks to capitalize on the privileged information that the order is coming to market. This practice is unethical and against the rules of the futures exchange.

19. Explain the difference in the roles of the National Futures Association and the Commodity Futures Trading Commission.

The National Futures Association (NFA) is an industry self–regulatory body, while the Commodity Futures Trading Commission (CFTC) is an agency of the federal government. The same law that instituted the CFTC also provided for the futures industry to establish self–regulatory bodies. The NFA enforces ethical standards on most futures industry members and provides testing for licensing of brokers and other futures industry professionals. The NFA operates under the supervision of the CFTC.

3

Futures Prices

Answers to Questions and Problems

1. Explain the function of the settlement committee. Why is the settlement price important in futures markets in a way that the day's final price in the stock market is not so important?

   In futures markets, the settlement committee determines the settlement price for each contract each day. The settlement price estimates the true value of the contract at the end of the day's trading. In active markets, the settlement price will typically equal the last trade price. In inactive markets, the settlement price is the committee's estimate of the price at which the contract would have traded at the close, if it had traded. The settlement price is important, because it is used to calculate margin requirements and the cash flows associated with daily settlement. In the stock market, there is no practice comparable to daily settlement, so the closing price in the stock market lacks the special significance of the futures settlement price.

2. Open interest tends to be low when a new contract expiration is first listed for trading, and it tends to be small after the contract has traded for a long time. Explain.

   When the contract is first listed for trading, open interest is necessarily zero. As traders take positions, the open interest builds. At expiration, open interest must again be zero. Every contract will have been fulfilled by offset, delivery, or an EFP. Therefore, as the contract approaches the expiration month, many traders will offset their positions to avoid delivery. This reduces open interest. In the expiration month, deliveries that occur further reduce open interest. Also, EFPs typically reduce open interest. This creates a pattern of very low open interest in the contract's early days of trading, followed by increases, followed by diminution, followed by the contract's extinction.

3. Explain the distinction between a normal and an inverted market.

   In a normal market, prices for more distant expirations are higher than prices for earlier expirations. In an inverted market, prices for more distant expirations are lower than prices for earlier expirations.

4. Explain why the futures price converges to the spot price and discuss what would happen if this convergence failed.

The explanation for convergence at expiration depends on whether the market features delivery or cash settlement, but in each case convergence depends on similar arbitrage arguments. We consider each type of contract in turn. For a contract with actual delivery, failure of convergence gives rise to an arbitrage opportunity at delivery. The cash price can be either above or below the futures price, if the two are not equal. If the cash price exceeds the futures price, the trader buys the future, accepts delivery, and sells the good in the cash market for the higher price. If the futures price exceeds the cash price, the trader buys the good on the cash market, sells a futures, and delivers the cash good in fulfillment of the futures. To exclude both types of arbitrage simultaneously, the futures price must equal the cash price at expiration. Minor discrepancies can exist, however. These are due to transaction costs and the fact that the short trader owns the options associated with initiating the delivery sequence.

For a contract with cash settlement, failure of convergence also implies arbitrage. Just before delivery, if the futures price exceeds the cash price a trader can sell the futures, wait for expiration, and the futures price will be set equal to the cash price. This gives a profit equal to the difference between the cash and futures. Alternatively, if the cash price is above the futures price, and expiration is imminent, the trader can buy the futures and wait for its price to be marked up to equal the cash price. Thus, no matter whether the futures price is above or below the cash price, a profit opportunity will be available immediately.

In short, the futures and cash price converge at expiration to exclude arbitrage, and failure of convergence implies the existence of arbitrage opportunities.

5. Is delivery, or the prospect of delivery, necessary to guarantee that the futures price will converge to the spot price? Explain.

No, delivery is not necessary. As explained in the answer to Question 4, cash settlement will also lead to convergence of the cash and the futures at expiration.

6. As we have defined the term, what are the two key elements of "academic arbitrage"?

The two elements are riskless profit and zero investment. Each condition is necessary for academic arbitrage, and the two conditions are jointly sufficient.

7. Assume that markets are perfect in the sense of being free from transaction costs and restrictions on short selling. The spot price of gold is $370. Current interest rates are 10 percent, compounded monthly. According to the Cost-of-Carry Model, what should the price of a gold futures contract be if expiration is six months away?

In perfect markets, the Cost-of-Carry Model gives the futures price as:

$$F_{0,t} = S_0(1 + C)$$

The cost of carrying gold for six months is $(1 + .10/12)^6 - 1 = .051053$. Therefore, the futures price should be:

$$F_{0,t} = \$370(1.051053) = \$388.89$$

8. Consider the information in Question 7. Round trip futures trading costs are $25 per 100 ounce gold contract, and buying or selling an ounce of gold incurs transaction costs of $1.25. Gold can be stored for $.15 per month per ounce. (Ignore interest on the storage fee and the transaction costs.) What futures prices are consistent with the Cost-of-Carry Model?

Answering this question requires finding the bounds imposed by the cash-and-carry and reverse cash-and-carry strategies. For convenience, we assume a transaction size of one 100-ounce contract. For the cash-and-carry the trader buys gold and sells the futures. This strategy requires the following cash outflows:

Buy gold	- $370(100)
Pay transaction costs on the spot	- $1.25(100)
Pay the storage cost	- $.15(100)(6)
Sell futures	0
Borrow to finance these outlays	+ $37,215

Six months later, the trader must:

Pay the transaction cost on one futures	- $25
Repay the borrowing	- $39,114.95
Deliver on futures	?

Net outlays at the outset were zero, and they were $39,139.95 at the horizon. Therefore, the futures price must exceed $391.40 an ounce for the cash-and-carry strategy to yield a profit.
The reverse cash-and-carry incurs the following cash flows. At the outset, the trader must:

Sell gold	+ $370(100)
Pay transaction costs on the spot	- $1.25(100)
Invest funds	- $36,875
Buy futures	0

These transactions provide a net zero initial cash flow. In six months, the trader has the following cash flows:

Collect on investment	$+ \$36,875(1 + .10/12)^6 = \$38,757.59$
Pay futures transaction costs	$- \$25$
Receive delivery on futures	?

The breakeven futures price is therefore $387.33 per ounce. Any lower price will generate a profit. From the cash-and-carry strategy, the futures price must be less than $391.40 to prevent arbitrage. From the reverse cash-and-carry strategy, the price must be at least $387.33. (Note that we assume there are no expenses associated with making or taking delivery.)

9.   Consider the information in Questions 7 and 8. Restrictions on short selling effectively mean that the reverse cash-and-carry trader in the gold market receives the use of only 90 percent of the value of the gold that is sold short. Based on this new information, what is the permissible range of futures prices?

This new assumption does not affect the cash-and-carry strategy, but it does limit the profitability of the reverse cash-and-carry trade. Specifically, the trader sells 100 ounces short but realizes only .9($370)(100) = $33,300 of usable funds. After paying the $125 spot transaction cost, the trader has $33,175 to invest. Therefore, the investment proceeds at the horizon are: $33,175(1 + .10/12)^6 = $34,868.69. Thus, all of the cash flows are:

Sell gold	$+ \$370(100)$
Pay transaction costs on the spot	$- \$1.25(100)$
Broker retains 10 percent	$- \$3,700$
Invest funds	$- \$33,175$
Buy futures	0

These transactions provide a net zero initial cash flow. In six months, the trader has the following cash flows:

Collect on investment	$34,868.69
Receive return of deposit from broker	$3,700
Pay futures transaction costs	$- \$25$
Receive delivery on futures	?

The breakeven futures price is therefore $385.44 per ounce. Any lower price will generate a profit. Thus, the no-arbitrage condition will be fulfilled if the futures price equals or exceeds $385.44 and equals or is less than $391.40.

10. Consider all of the information about gold in Questions 7-9. The interest rate in Question 7 is 10 percent per annum, with monthly compounding. This is the borrowing rate. Lending brings only 8 percent, compounded monthly. What is the permissible range of futures prices when we consider this imperfection as well?

    The lower lending rate reduces the proceeds from the reverse cash-and-carry strategy. Now the trader has the following cash flows:

Sell gold	+ $370(100)
Pay transaction costs on the spot	- $1.25(100)
Broker retains 10 percent	- $3,700
Invest funds	- $33,175
Buy futures	0

    These transactions provide a net zero initial cash flow. Now the investment will yield only $33,175(1 + .08/12)^6 = $34,524.31$. In six months, the trader has the following cash flows:

Collect on investment	$34,524.31
Pay futures transaction costs	- $25
Receive delivery on futures	?
Return gold to close short sale	0
Receive return of deposit from broker	$ 3,700

    Total proceeds on the 100 ounces are $38,199.31. Therefore, the futures price per ounce must be less than $381.99 for the reverse cash-and-carry strategy to profit. Because the borrowing rate has not changed, the bound from the cash-and-carry strategy remains at $391.40. Therefore, the futures price must remain within the inclusive bounds of $381.99 to $391.40 to exclude arbitrage.

11. Consider all of the information about gold in Questions 7-10. The gold futures expiring in six months trades for $375 per ounce. Explain how you would respond to this price given all of the market imperfections we have considered. Show your transactions in a table similar to Tables 3.8 or 3.9. Answer the same question, assuming that gold trades for $395.

    If the futures price is $395, it exceeds the bound imposed by the cash-and- carry strategy and it should be possible to trade as follows:

Cash-and-Carry Arbitrage

$t = 0$		
	Borrow $37,215 for 6 months at 10%.	+ $37,215.00
	Buy 100 ounces of spot gold.	- 37,000.00
	Pay storage costs for 6 months.	- 90.00
	Pay transaction costs on gold purchase.	- 125.00
	Sell futures for $395.	0.00
		Total Cash Flow $0
$t = 6$	Remove gold from storage.	$0
	Deliver gold on futures.	+ 39,500.00
	Pay futures transaction cost.	- 25.00
	Repay debt.	- 39,114.95
		Total Cash Flow + $360.05

If the futures price is $375, the reverse cash-and-carry strategy should generate a profit as follows:

Reverse Cash-and-Carry Arbitrage

$t = 0$		
	Sell 100 ounces of gold short.	+ $37,000.00
	Pay transaction costs.	- 125.00
	Broker retains 10%.	-3,700.00
	Buy futures.	0
	Invest remaining funds for 6 months at 8%.	-33,175.00
		Total Cash Flow $0
$t = 6$	Collect on investment.	+ $34,524.31
	Receive delivery on futures.	-37,500.00
	Return gold to close short sale.	0
	Receive return of deposit from broker.	+ 3,700.00
	Pay futures transaction cost.	- 25.00
		Total Cash Flow + $699.31

12. Explain the difference between pure and quasi-arbitrage.

   In a pure arbitrage transaction, the arbitrageur faces full transaction costs on each transaction comprising the arbitrage. For example, a retail customer with no initial position in the market, who attempts arbitrage, would be attempting pure arbitrage. By contrast, a quasi-arbitrage transaction occurs when a trader faces less than full transaction costs. The most common example arises in reverse cash-and-carry arbitrage, which requires short selling. For example, in stock index arbitrage, holding a large portfolio allows a trader to simulate a short sale by selling part of the portfolio from inventory. Therefore, this trader faces less than the full transaction costs due to the pre-existing position in the market. By contrast, the pure arbitrage trade would require the actual short sale of the stocks, and short selling does not provide the full proceeds to earn interest in the reverse cash-and-carry transactions.

13. Assume that you are a gold merchant with an ample supply of deliverable gold. Explain how you can simulate short selling and compute the price of gold that will bring you into the market for reverse cash-and-carry arbitrage.

   The breakeven price for reverse cash-and-carry arbitrage depends principally on the transaction costs the trader faces. With an existing inventory of gold, the trader can simulate short selling by selling a portion of the inventory. Further, because the trader already actually owns the gold, she can have full use of the proceeds of the sale. Therefore, the gold owner's reverse cash-and-carry transactions are similar to those in Problem 10:

Reverse Cash-and-Carry Arbitrage

$t = 0$	Sell 100 ounces of gold short.	+ $37,000.00
	Pay transaction costs.	- 125.00
	Buy futures.	0
	Invest funds for 6 months at 8%.	- 36,875.00
		Total Cash Flow $0
$t = 6$	Collect on investment.	+ $38,374.80
	Return gold to close short sale.	0
	Pay futures transaction cost.	- 25.00
	Receive delivery on futures.	
	(Note: This is the futures price	- 38,349.80
	to give zero cash flow.)	
		Total Cash Flow + $0

Therefore, if the futures price is $383.498 per ounce, the reverse cash-and- carry transactions give a zero cash flow. This is the breakeven price for reverse cash-and-carry. If the futures price is less that $383.498 per ounce, reverse cash-and-carry arbitrage will be possible for the trader who holds an initial inventory of gold. In Problem 10, the price of gold has to be less than $381.99 for reverse cash-and-carry arbitrage to work. The trader there faced full transaction costs, due to a lack of a pre-existing inventory.

14. Assume that silver trades in a full carry market. If the spot price is $5.90 per ounce and the futures that expires in one year trades for $6.55, what is the implied cost-of-carry? Under what conditions would it be appropriate to regard this implied cost-of-carry as an implied repo rate?

   If the market is at full carry, then $F_{0,t} = S_0(1 + C)$ and $C = F_{0,t}/S_0 - 1$. With our values, $C = $6.55/$5.90 - 1 = .110169$. It would be appropriate to regard this implied cost-of-carry as an implied repo rate if the only carrying cost were the financing cost. This is approximately true for silver.

15. What is "normal backwardation"? What might give rise to normal backwardation?

   Normal backwardation is the view that futures prices normally rise over their life. Thus, prices are expected to rise as expiration approaches. The classic argument for normal backwardation stems from Keynes. According to Keynes, hedgers are short in the aggregate, so speculators must be net long. Speculators provide their risk-bearing services for an expected profit. To have an expected profit, the futures price must be less than the expected future spot price at the time the speculators assume their long positions. Therefore, given unbiased expectations regarding future spot prices, we expect futures prices to rise over time to give the speculators their compensation. This leads directly to normal backwardation.

16. Assume that the CAPM beta of a futures contract is zero, but that the price of this commodity tends to rise over time very consistently. Interpret the implications of this evidence for normal backwardation and for the CAPM.

   Because futures trading requires no investment, positive returns on long futures positions can be consistent with the CAPM only if futures have positive betas. With a zero beta (by our assumption) and a zero investment to acquire a long futures position (by the structure of the market), the CAPM implies zero expected returns. Therefore, a zero beta and positive returns is inconsistent with the CAPM. Even with zero beta, positive returns are consistent with normal backwardation resulting from speculators assuming long positions and being rewarded for their risk-bearing services.

17. Explain why futures and forward prices might differ. Assume that platinum prices are positively correlated with interest rates. What should be the relationship between platinum forward and futures prices? Explain.

Futures are subject to daily settlement cash flows, while forwards are not. If the price of the underlying good is not correlated with interest rates, futures and forward prices will be equal. If the price of the underlying good is positively correlated with interest rates, a long trader in futures will receive daily settlement cash inflows when interest rates are high and the trader can invest that cash flow at the higher rate from the time of receipt to the expiration of the futures. Because forwards have no daily settlement cash flows, they are unable to reap this benefit. Therefore, if a commodity's price is positively correlated with interest rates, there will be an advantage to a futures over a forward. Thus, for platinum in the question, the futures price of platinum should exceed the forward price. The opposite price relationship can occur if there is negative correlation. Generally, this price relationship is not sufficiently strong to be observed in the market.

18. Consider the life of a futures contract from inception to delivery. Explain two fundamental theories on why the futures prices might exhibit different volatility at different times over the life of the contract.

According to the Samuelson hypothesis, price volatility will be greater when more information about the price of the good is being revealed. According to this view, this tends to happen as the futures comes to expiration, particularly for agricultural goods. Therefore, the Samuelson hypothesis suggests that the volatility of futures prices should increase over the life of the contract.

There are several other theories that attempt to relate contract maturity and volatility. First, there seems to be some evidence for believing that volatility is higher for some commodities in certain seasons, particularly at times when information about the harvest of some good is reaching the market. With this view, volatility depends on the time of the year and not so much on the contract's expiration. Second, volatility also differs depending on the day of the week. Third, volatility is autocorrelated. High volatility in one month begets high volatility in the next month.

4
Using Futures Markets

Answers to Questions and Problems

1. Explain how futures markets can benefit individuals in society who never trade futures.

    One of the main benefits that the futures market provides is price discovery; futures markets provide information about the likely future price of commodities. This information is available to anyone in the economy, because the prices are publicly available. It is not necessary to trade futures to reap this benefit.

2. A "futures price" is a market quoted price today of the best estimate of the value of a commodity at the expiration of the futures contract. What do you think of this definition?

    This claim is intriguing but controversial. If there is no risk premium imbedded in the futures price, the statement is likely to be true. The definition implies that random holding of futures positions should earn a zero profit. This seems to be approximately true, but studies such as that by Bodie and Rosansky find positive returns to long futures positions. While the claim may not hold literally, it does seem to be close to correct. Further, those who reject the claim may have a difficult time in identifying futures prices that are above or below the future spot price.

3. Explain the concept of an unbiased predictor.

    A predictor is unbiased if the average prediction error equals zero. This implies that errors in the prediction are distributed around zero, and that the prediction is equally likely to be high as well as low.

4. How are errors possible if a predictor is unbiased?

    Saying that a predictor is unbiased merely claims that the predictions do not tend to be too high or too low. They can still be in error. For example, the futures price may provide an unbiased prediction of the future spot price of a commodity. Nonetheless, the errors in such a prediction are often large, because the futures price today can diverge radically from the spot price at the expiration of the futures.

5.   Scalpers trade to capture profits from minute fluctuations in futures prices. Explain how this avaricious behavior benefits others.

Scalpers trade frequently, attempting to profit by a tick here or there. In pursuing their profit, the scalpers provide the market with liquidity. Thus, a trader who wishes to take or offset a position benefits from the presence of scalpers ready to take the opposite side of the transaction. With many scalpers competing for business, position traders will be able to trade at prices that closely approximate the true value of the commodity. Expressed another way, as scalpers compete for profits, they force the bid/asked spread to narrow, therefore contributing to the liquidity of the market.

6.   Assume that scalping is made illegal. What would the consequences of such an action be for hedging activity in futures markets?

Without scalpers, the liquidity of the futures market would be greatly impaired. This would imply a widening of bid/asked spreads. The potential hedger would face having to accept a price that was distant from the true price. Faced with the higher transaction costs represented by wider bid/asked spreads, some hedgers might find that hedging is too expensive and they might not hedge. Thus, without scalpers hedging would be more expensive, and we would observe a lower volume of hedging activity.

7.   A trader anticipates rising corn prices and wants to take advantage of this insight by trading an intra-commodity spread. Would you advise that she trade long nearby/short distant or the other way around? Explain.

The answer depends on the relative responsiveness to nearby and distant futures prices to a generally rising price level for corn. If the nearby contract price rises more than the price of the distant contract, the trader should go long nearby/short distant, for example. For most agricultural commodities there is no general rule to follow.

8.   Assume that daily settlement prices in the futures market exhibit very strong first order serial correlation. How would you trade to exploit this strategy? Explain how your answer would differ if the correlation is statistically significant but, nonetheless, small in magnitude.

With strong serial correlation, a price rise is likely to be followed by another price rise, and a price drop is likely to be followed by another price drop. Therefore, the trader should buy after a price rise and sell after a price fall. If the correlation is strong, the strategy should generate profits. However, the correlation must be very strong to generate profits sufficient to cover transaction costs. The correlation can be statistically significant, but still too small to be economically significant. To be economically significant the correlation must be strong enough to generate trading profits that will cover the transaction costs. Studies typically find statistically significant first order serial correlation in futures price changes, but they also find that these correlations are not economically significant.

9. Assume that you are a rabid efficient markets believer. A commodity fund uses 20 percent of its funds as margin payments. The remaining 80 percent are invested in risk-free securities. What investment performance would you expect from the fund?

For any efficient markets believer, rabid or calm, the expected return on the 80 percent of the funds is the risk-free rate. If there is no risk premium, the expected profit on the futures position is zero. Thus, we define a rabid efficient markets believer as one who denies the existence of a risk premium. Therefore, the rabid theorist expects returns from the funds that would be 80 percent of the risk-free rate.

10. Consider two traders. The first trader is an individual with his own seat who trades strictly for his own account. The other trader works for a brokerage firm actively engaged in retail futures brokerage. Which trader has a lower effective marginal trading cost? Relate this comparison in marginal trading costs to quasi-arbitrage.

This is a difficult question. The trader who owns a seat incurs the following costs to trade: the capital commitment to the seat, the opportunity cost of foregone alternative employment, and the exchange member's out-of-pocket transaction costs. These out-of-pocket costs are quite low. For the broker, the scale is much greater. Behind the broker in the pit stands the entire brokerage firm organization with the overhead it represents. Offsetting this overhead to some extent is the much greater scale associated with the brokerage firm. Also, for the trader associated with the brokerage firm, much of the overhead is associated with retail operations, and the marginal cost of trading an additional contract can be quite low. Thus, we judge that the brokerage firm has the lower marginal cost of trading. This difference in trading costs (whichever is really lower) can be important for quasi-arbitrage. Essentially, the fruits of quasi-arbitrage can be harvested by the trader with the lowest marginal transaction costs. If our assessment of these costs is correct, the brokerage firm should be able to squeeze out the market maker and capture these quasi-arbitrage profits.

11. Consider the classic hedging problems of the farmer who sells wheat in the futures market in anticipation of a harvest. Would the farmer be likely to deliver his harvested wheat against the futures? Explain. If he is unlikely to deliver, explain how he manages his futures position instead.

Most farmers that hedge would not deliver against the futures. Often the wheat would not be deliverable, due to differences in grade or type of wheat. Also, the wheat is probably distant from an approved delivery point, and trying to deliver the wheat would involve prohibitively high transportation costs. Instead of actually delivering, the farmer would be much more likely to sell the harvested wheat to the local grain elevator and offset the futures position.

12. A cocoa merchant holds a current inventory of cocoa worth $10 million at present prices of $1,250 per metric ton. The standard deviation of returns for the inventory is .27. She is considering a risk-minimization hedge of her inventory using the cocoa contract of the Coffee, Cocoa and Sugar Exchange. The contract size is 10 metric tons. The volatility of the futures is .33. For the particular grade of cocoa in her inventory, the correlation between the futures and spot cocoa is .85. Compute the risk-minimization hedge ratio and determine how many contracts she should trade.

We know that the hedge ratio is:

$$HR = \frac{\rho_{SF}\, \sigma_S\, \sigma_F}{\sigma_F^2}$$

where S and F indicate the spot and futures, respectively. Therefore, with our data, the hedge ratio is:

$$HR = \frac{\rho_{SF}\, \sigma_S\, \sigma_F}{\sigma_F^2} = \frac{.85\,(.27)\,(.33)}{(.33)\,(.33)} = .6955$$

Currently, the merchant holds $10,000,000/$1,250 = 8,000 metric tons. The hedge ratio indicates trading .6955 of the futures for each unit of the spot. This implies a futures position of 8,000(.6955) = 5,563.64 metric tons. With the futures consisting of 10 tons per contract, the correct futures quantity is 5,564/10 ≈ 56 contracts. Because she is long the physical cocoa, she should sell 56 futures contracts.

13. A service station operator read this book. He wants to hedge his risk exposure for gasoline. Every week, he pumps 50,000 gallons of gasoline, and he is confident that this pattern will hold through thick and Hussein. What advice would you offer?

The operator should probably not hedge. By construction, the operator faces a fairly small and recurring risk. If the futures price equals the expected future spot price, the expected gains from hedging are zero, ignoring transaction costs. If we consider transaction costs, the hedging program is almost certain to cost money over the long run. Futures hedging is better designed for large risks or special applications. Persistent hedging of repeated small and independent risks will lead to losses equal to the transaction costs the more often the hedge is attempted (assuming the futures price equals the expected future spot price).

5
Interest Rate Futures: Introduction

Answers to Questions and Problems

1. A 90-day T-bill yields 8.75 percent. What is the price of a $1,000,000 face value bill?

   Applying the equation for the value of a T-bill, the price of a $1,000,000 face value T-bill is $1,000,000 - DY($1,000,000)(DTM)/360, where DY is the discount yield and DTM = days until maturity. Therefore, if DY = .0875 the bill price is:

   $$\text{Bill Price} = \$1,000,000 - \frac{.0835\,(\$1,000,000)\,(90)}{360} = \$979,125$$

2. The IMM Index stands as 88.70. What is the discount yield? If you buy a T-bill futures at that index value and the index becomes 88.90, what is your gain or loss?

   The discount yield = 100.00 - IMM Index = 100.00 - 88.70 = 11.30 percent. If the IMM Index moves to 88.90, it has gained 20 basis points, and each point is worth $25. Because the price has risen and the yield has fallen, the long position has a profit of $25(20) = $500.

3. What is the difference between Position Day and First Position Day?

   First Position Day is the first day on which a trader can initiate the delivery sequence on CBOT futures contracts. With the three day delivery sequence characteristics of T-bond futures, for example, First Position Day is the second to last business day of the month preceding the contract's expiration month. For example, May 30 is the first position day for the JUN contract, assuming that May 30-June 1 are all business days. Position Day is functionally the same, but it is not the first day on which a trader can initiate the sequence. For example, assuming June 10-12 are all business days, the Position Day could be June 10, with actual delivery occurring on June 12.

4. A $100,000 face value T-bond has an annual coupon rate of 9.5 percent and paid its last coupon 48 days ago. What is the accrued interest on the bond?

    Accrued Interest = $100,000 (.095/2)(48/182.5) = $1,249.32.

    Note that we assume that the half-year has 182.5 days. There are specific rules for determining the number of days in a half-year.

5. What conditions are necessary for the conversion factors on the CBOT T-bond contract to create favorable conditions for delivering one bond instead of another?

    There is one market condition under which the conversion factor method creates no bias: the yield curve is flat and all rates are 8 percent. Under any other circumstance, the conversion factor method will give incentives to deliver some bonds in preference to others.

6. The Municipal Bond Index futures does not allow for delivery of bonds. Explain why the futures price must converge to the spot index value nonetheless.

    The MBI uses cash settlement, so at expiration the final settlement price on the futures is set equal to the cash index value. This guarantees exact convergence at expiration. Prior to expiration, deviations between futures prices and the spot index will create arbitrage opportunities. If the futures price is too high relative to the spot index value, there will be cash-and-carry arbitrage opportunities. If the futures price is too low relative to the spot index, there will be reverse cash-and-carry arbitrage opportunities.

7. The JUN T-bill futures IMM Index value is 92.80, while the SEP has a value of 93.00. What is the implied rate to cover the period from June to September?

    For the JUN contract the implied invoice amount is:

    Bill Price = $1,000,000 - .0720($1,000,000)(90)/360 = $982,000

    Paying this amount in June will yield $1,000,000 in September when the delivered T-bill matures. Therefore, the implied interest rate is:

    $$\text{Implied Yield} = \left(\frac{\$1,000,000}{\$980,000} \right)^4 - 1 = .084166$$

Therefore, the implied annual interest rate to cover the June-September period is 8.4166 percent. (The information about the SEP futures is just a distraction.)

8. A spot 180-day T-bill has a discount yield of 9.5 percent. If the implied repo rate for the next three months is 9.2 percent, what is the price of a futures that expires in three months?

   To exclude arbitrage, the strategy of holding the 180-day T-bill must give the same return as investing for the first three months at the repo rate and taking delivery on the futures to cover the second three month period to make up the 180-day holding period.
      Assuming $1,000,000 face values, the price of the 180-day bill must be:

$$\text{Bill Price} = \$1,000,000 - .095(\$1,000,000)(180)/360 = \$952,500$$

   The futures price must be $\$952,500(1.092)^{.25} = \$973,690$ to exclude arbitrage. This dollar price for the futures implies a discount yield of .10524:

$$DY = [(360/90)(\$1,000,000 - \$973,690)]/\$1,000,000 = .10524$$

   This discount yield in turn implies an IMM Index value of 89.48.

9. For the next three futures expirations, you observe the following Eurodollar quotations:

MAR	92.00
JUN	91.80
SEP	91.65

   What shape does the yield curve have? Explain.

   These IMM Index values imply Eurodollar add-on yields of 8 percent, 8.2 percent, and 8.35 percent, respectively. These rates apply to the following periods: March-June, June-September, and September-December, respectively. Essentially, we may regard these futures rates as forward rates. If forward rates increase with futurity, the yield curve must be upward sloping.

10. Assume that the prices in the preceding problem pertain to T-bill futures and the MAR contract expires today. What should be the spot price of an 180-day T-bill?

    To avoid arbitrage, the spot price of an 180-day T-bill must give the same return as taking delivery on the futures today and taking a long position in the JUN contract with the intention of taking delivery of it as well. For convenience, we assume a T-bill with a face value of $1,000,000.

With the strategy of two 90-day positions, a trader would need to take delivery of both one full JUN contract and enough bills on the MAR contract to pay the invoice amount on the JUN contract. For the JUN contract, the IMM Index value implies a delivery price of $1,000,000 - .0820($1,000,000)(90)/360 = $979,500. For the MAR contract, the delivery price is $1,000,000 - .08($1,000,000)(90)/360 = $980,000. But the trader requires only $979,500 (or 97.95 percent) of the JUN contract. Therefore, for the short-term strategy, the current price of $1,000,000 in September is .9795($980,000) = $959,910. To avoid arbitrage, the 180-day bill must also cost $959,910, implying a discount yield of .08018.

11. The cheapest-to-deliver T-bond is a 12 percent bond that paid its coupon 87 days ago and is priced at 105-16. The conversion factor of the bond is 1.0900. The nearby T-bond futures expires in 50 days and the current price is 98-00. If you can borrow or lend to finance a T-bond for a total outlay of 2 percent over this period, how would you transact? What if you could borrow or lend at 3 percent? What if you could borrow at 3 percent and lend at 2 percent? Explain.

To know how to respond to these quotations requires knowing the invoice amount that can be obtained for the bond and comparing this with the cost of carrying the bond to delivery on the futures. For convenience, we assume a face value that equals the contract size of $100,000. First, the accrued interest (assuming a 182.5-day half-year) is:

$$AI = (87/182.5)(.5)(.12)\$100,000 = \$2,860.27$$

At expiration, the accrued interest will be:

$$AI = (137/182.5)(.5)(.12)\$100,000 = \$4,504.11$$

For this bond and the futures price of 98-00, the invoice amount will be:

$$\text{Invoice Amount} = .9800(\$100,000)(1.09) + \$4,504.11 = \$111,324.11$$

Buying the bond and carrying it to delivery (at 2 percent interest for the period) costs:

$$(\$105,500 + \$2,860.27)(1.02) = \$110,527.48$$

Because the cost of acquiring and carrying the bond to delivery is less than the expected invoice amount, the trader could engage in a cash-and-carry arbitrage. Buying the bond and carrying it to delivery costs $110,527.48 and nets a cash inflow of $111,324.11. This gives an arbitrage profit. (Notice that the actual invoice amount is unknown, but transacting at the futures price of 98-00 guarantees the profit we have computed. This profit may be realized earlier depending upon the daily settlement cash flows.)

If the cost of carrying the bond for these next 50 days is 3 percent instead of 2 percent, the total cost of acquiring and carrying the bond will not work. The total outlay will be:

$$(\$105,500 + \$2,860.27)(1.03) = \$111,611.08$$

Ignoring the short seller's options to choose the deliverable bond and the delivery date within the delivery month, the following reverse cash-and-carry strategy will be available with the 3 percent financing rate. The trader can buy the futures, borrow the bond and sell it short, and invest the proceeds to earn $111,611.08 by delivery. The short, we assume, obligingly delivers the same bond on the right day for the invoice amount of $111,324.11, and the profit is: $111,611.08 - $111,324.11 = $286.97.

If the trader can borrow at 3 percent and lend at 2 percent, these prices create no arbitrage opportunities. The cash-and-carry strategy is too expensive, because buying and carrying the bond costs $111,611.08, more than the invoice amount of $111,324.11. The reverse cash-and-carry strategy is also impractical, because it nets only $110,527.48, less than the invoice amount of $111,324.11.

12. You expect a steepening yield curve over the next few months, but you are not sure whether the level of rates will increase or decrease. Explain two different ways you can trade to profit if you are correct.

If the yield curve is to steepen, distant rates must rise relative to nearby rates. If this happens we can exploit the event by trading just short-term instruments. The yield on distant expiration short-term instruments must rise relative to the yield on nearby expiration short-term instruments. Therefore, one should sell the distant expiration and buy the nearby expiration. This strategy could be implemented by trading Eurodollar or T-bill futures.

As a second basic technique, one could trade longer term T-bonds against shorter maturity T-notes. Here the trader expects yields on T-bonds to rise relative to yields on T-notes. Therefore, the trader should sell T-bond futures and buy T-note futures. Here the two different contracts can have the same expiration month.

13. The Iraqi invasion of Alaska has financial markets in turmoil. You expect the crisis to worsen more than other traders suspect. How could you trade short-term interest rate futures to profit if you are correct? Explain.

Greater than expected turmoil might be expected to result in rising yields on interest rate futures. To exploit this event, a trader could sell futures outright. A second result might be an increasing risk premium on short-term instruments. In this case, the yield differential between Eurodollar and T-bill futures might increase. To exploit this event, the trader could sell Eurodollar futures and buy T-bill futures of the same maturity.

14. You believe that the yield curve is strongly upward sloping and that yields are at very high levels. How would you use interest rate futures to hedge a prospective investment of funds that you will receive in nine months? If you faced a major borrowing in nine months, how would you use futures?

 If you think yields are near their peak, you will want to lock-in these favorable rates for the investment of funds that you will receive. Therefore, you should buy futures that will expire at about the time you will receive your funds. The question does not suggest whether you will be investing long-term or short-term. However, if the yield curve is strongly upward sloping, it might favor longer term investment. Consequently, you might buy T-bond futures expiring in about nine months.

 If you expect to borrow funds in nine months you may not want to use the futures market at all. In the question, we assume that you believe rates are unsustainably high. Trading to lock-in these rates only ensures that your borrowing takes place at the currently very high effective rates. Given your beliefs, it might be better to speculate on falling rates.

15. The spot rate of interest on a corporate bond is 11 percent, and the yield curve is sharply upward sloping. The futures rate on the T-bond futures that is just about to expire is 8 percent, but the yield for the futures contract that expires in six months is 8.75 percent. (You are convinced that this difference is independent of any difference in the cheapest-to-deliver bonds for the two contracts.) In these circumstances, a corporate finance officer wants to lock-in the current spot rate of 11 percent on a corporate bond that her firm plans to offer in six months. What advice would you give her?

 Reform your desires to conform to reality. The yield curve is upward sloping and the spot corporate rate is 11 percent. Therefore, the forward corporate rate implied by the yield curve must exceed 11 percent. Trading futures now to lock-in a rate for the future locks in the rate implied by the yield curve, and that rate will exceed 11 percent. Consequently, she must expect to lock in a rate above the current spot rate of 11 percent.

6

Interest Rate Futures: Refinements

Answers to Questions and Problems

Assume today is January 30, 1992. You are considering two bonds as potential bonds for delivery against the JUN 92 T-bond futures contract, which settled at 102-08. First is the 7¼ bond that matures on May 15, 2016. Second, you might deliver the 13¼ bond that matures on May 15, 2014, but is callable on May 15, 2009. Use this information for Questions 1-8.

1. Using the facts outlined above, find the conversion factors for the two bonds for the JUN 92 futures contract.

    For the conversion factor, the critical date for the JUN 92 contract is June 1, 1992, the first possible delivery date. On that date, the bond that matures in 2016 will have its next payment in November 1992 and its second payment in May 1993. This means that it will have an even number of payments, because the May payment is an even payment and the bond expires in May. Therefore, the bond maturing in 2016 has 48 payments remaining until maturity. The bond of 2009-2014 matures in 2014 but is callable in 2009. The first call date is key for the T-bond futures delivery. On June 1, 1992, there will be 34 payments to first call. To find the conversion factors, we use the following equation from the text for an even number of payments.

    $$CF = \sum_{t=1}^{n} \frac{C_t}{1.04^t} + \frac{1}{1.04^n}$$

    Applying this equation for the bond of 2016 gives:

    $$CF = \sum_{t=1}^{48} \frac{.03625}{1.04^t} + \frac{1}{1.04^{48}} = .7683 + .1522 = .9205$$

    For the bond callable in 2009, we have:

$$CF = \sum_{t=1}^{34} \frac{.06625}{1.04^{\,t}} + \frac{1}{1.04^{\,34}} = 1.2197 + .2636 = 1.4833$$

2. On January 30, 1992, what is the accrued interest on each bond?

On January 30, both bonds are in the November-May half-year. For interest paid on the 15th in a leap year, the half-year has 182 days according to the table from the text. Since the last payment on November 15, 76 days have elapsed (15 in November, 31 in December, and 30 in January.) Assuming a $100,000 face value, we have the following accrued interest.

For the 7¼ bond: AI = (76/182) $3,625 = $1,513.74

For the 13¼ bond: AI = (76/182) $6,625 = $2,766.48

3. Consider a position day of June 15, 1992. What is the accrued interest on each bond?

On June 15, 1992, we are in the May-November half-year. In a leap year for a bond paying on the 15th, the half-year is 184 days. Since the last payment on May 15, 31 days have elapsed.

For the 7¼ bond: AI = (31/184) $3,625 = $610.73

For the 13¼ bond: AI = (31/184) $6,625 = $1,116.17

4. Assuming the settlement price on position day (June 15, 1992) is 114-00, find the invoice amounts for both bonds.

From the text, we know:

$$\text{Invoice Amount} = \text{DSP}\ (\$100,000)\ (\text{CF}) + \text{AI}$$

For the 7¼ bond:

$$\text{Invoice Amount} = 1.14\ (\$100,000)(.9205) + \$610.73 = \$105,547.73$$

For the 13¼ bond:

$$\text{Invoice Amount} = 1.14\ (\$100,000)(1.4833) + \$1,116.17 = \$170,212.37$$

5. The 7¼ bond trades for 85-00 and the 13¼ is at 137-00. Which bond do you expect to be cheaper to deliver? (Assume a financing rate of 8 percent.)

From January 30 to delivery on June 15, 1992, there is an intervening coupon payment. The profit from delivery is:

$$\pi = DFP_0(CF) + AI_2 - \{(P_0 + AI_0)(1 + C_{0,2}) - COUP_1(1 + C_{1,2})\}$$

The present is January 30, the coupon date is May 15, and the delivery date is June 15. These dates are $t = 0$, $t = 1$, and $t = 2$, respectively. From $t = 0$ to $t = 1$ is 106 days (January has 1, February has 29, March has 31, April has 30, and May has 15). From $t = 1$ to $t = 2$ is 31 days. Therefore, the interest factor from $t = 0$ to $t = 1$ is $1 + (106/360).08 = 1.0236$, and from $t = 1$ to $t = 2$ it is $1 + (31/360).08 = 1.0069$. From $t = 0$ to $t = 2$, there are 137 days and the interest factor is $1 + (137/360).08 = 1.0304$.

Applying the equation to the 7¼ bond we have:

$$\pi = DFP_0(CF) + AI_2 - \{(P_0 + AI_0)(1 + C_{0,2}) - COUP_1(1 + C_{1,2})\}$$

$$= \$102,250(.9205) + \$610.73 - \{(\$85,000 + \$1513.74)(1.0304)$$

$$- \$3,625(1.0069)\}$$

$$= \$94,121.13 + \$610.73 - \{\$89,143.76 - \$3,650.01\} = \$9,238.11$$

Applying the equation to the 13¼ bond we have:

$$\pi = DFP_0(CF) + AI_2 - \{(P_0 + AI_0)(1 + C_{0,2}) - COUP_1(1 + C_{1,2})\}$$

$$= \$102,250(1.4833) + \$1,116.17 - \{(\$137,000 + \$2,766.48)(1.0304)$$

$$- \$6,625(1.0069)\}$$

$$= \$151,667.43 + \$1,116.17 - \{\$144,015.38 - \$6,670.71\}$$

$$= \$15,438.93$$

The expected profit from delivering the 7¼ is $9,238.11, but the expected profit from delivering the 13¼ is $15,438.93. Therefore, we expect the 13¼ to be cheaper to deliver.

6. Assume that between now (January 30, 1992) and delivery on June 15, 1992, that you can finance a cash-and-carry transaction at 8 percent. This is your borrowing and lending rate. Further assume that you have full use of all short sale proceeds. Find all possible arbitrage strategies.

From Problem 5, both bonds would offer cash-and-carry arbitrage profits. For the 7¼ bond the transactions are as follows:

For the 7¼ Bond

January 30, 1992

Sell the JUN 92 T-bond futures at 102-08.	$0
Borrow $86,513.74 for 137 days at 8%.	+ 86,513.74
Buy $100,000 face value of the 7¼ bond paying $85,000 plus accrued interest of $1,513.74.	- 86,513.74
	Total Cash Flow $0

May 15, 1992

Receive coupon.	+ $3,625.00
Lend coupon amount for 31 days at 8%.	- 3,625.00
	Total Cash Flow $0

June 15, 1992 (Assume futures is still at 102-08 for convenience only.)

Deliver bond and receive invoice amount of $102,250(.9205) + $610.73.	+ $94,731.86
Collect on invested coupon: ($3,625)(1.0069).	+ 3,650.01
Repay debt incurred on Jan. 30: $86,513.74(1.0304).	- 89,143.76
	Total Cash Flow $9,238.11

For the 13¼ bond the transactions are as follows:

For the 13¼ Bond	
January 30, 1992	
Sell the JUN 92 T-bond futures at 102-08.	$0
Borrow $139,766.48 for 137 days at 8%.	+ 139,766.48
Buy $100,000 face value of the 13¼ bond paying $137,000 plus accrued interest of $2,766.48.	- 139,766.48
	Total Cash Flow $0
May 15, 1992	
Receive coupon.	+ $6,625.00
Lend coupon amount for 31 days at 8%.	- 6,625.00
	Total Cash Flow $0
June 15, 1992 (Assume futures is still at 102-08 for convenience only.)	
Deliver bond and receive invoice amount of $102,250(1.4833) + $1,116.17.	+ $152,783.60
Collect on invested coupon: ($6,625)(1.0069).	+ 6,670.71
Repay debt incurred on Jan. 30: $139,766.48(1.0304).	- 144,015.38
	Total Cash Flow $15,438.93

We assume that the futures price on June 15 is 102-08, the same price as our original sale price. This simplification abstracts from daily settlement cash flows. For any ending futures price, the profit will be the same, assuming that we ignore the interest that might be earned or paid on the daily settlement cash flows.

7. Find the implied repo rates for both bonds.

In terms of our notation:

Implied Repo Rate =

$$\frac{DFP_0 \, (100{,}000) \, (CF) + AI_2 + COUP_1 \, (1 + C_{1,2}) - (P_0 + AI_0)}{(P_0 + AI_0)}$$

Applying this equation to the 7¼ bond gives:

$$= \frac{\$94,121 + \$610.73 + \$3,625(1.0069) - (\$85,000 + \$1,513.74)}{\$85,000 + \$1,513.74}$$

$$= .1373$$

For the 13¼ bond, the equation gives:

$$= \frac{\$151,667 + \$1,116.17 + \$6,625(1.0069) - (\$137,000 + \$2,766.48)}{\$137,000 + \$2,766.48}$$

$$= .1409$$

The implied repo rates are 13.73 percent for the 7¼ bond and 14.09 percent for the 13¼ bonds. These are not annualized but are the rates for the period from January 30 to June 15.

8. Continue to assume that you can borrow and lend at 8 percent. However, now you can use only 90 percent of any short sale proceeds on a reverse cash-and-carry strategy. How does this change your trading strategy, if at all?

    This assumption has no effect, because both bonds offered a cash-and-carry opportunity, and there was no chance for a reverse cash-and-carry trade.

9. Explain the risks inherent in a reverse cash-and-carry strategy in the T-bond futures market.

    The reverse cash-and-carry strategy requires waiting to receive delivery. However, the delivery options all rest with the short trader. The short trader will initiate delivery at his or her convenience. In the T-bond market, this exposes the reverse cash-and-carry trader to receiving delivery at some time other than the date planned. Also, with so many different deliverable bonds, the reverse cash-and-carry trader is unlikely to receive the bond he or she desires. (These factors are fairly common for other commodities as well.) In the T-bond futures market, the short trader holds some special options such as the wildcard and end-of-month options. The reverse cash-and-carry trader suffers the risk that the short trader will find it advantageous to exploit the wildcard play or exercise the end-of-month option.

10. Explain how the concepts of quasi-arbitrage help to overcome the risks inherent in reverse cash-and-carry trading in T-bond futures.

   In pure reverse cash-and-carry arbitrage, the trader sells the bond short and buys the future. The trader thereby suffers risk about which bond will be delivered and the time at which it will be delivered. If the trader holds a large portfolio of bonds and sells some bond from inventory to simulate the short sale, these risks are mitigated. Receiving a particular bond on delivery is no longer so crucial to the trader's cash flows; after all, whichever bond is delivered will merely supplement the trader's portfolio. Further, the timing of delivery presents fewer problems to the quasi-arbitrage trader. In selling a bond from inventory, as opposed to an actual short sale, the trader did not need to worry about financing the short sale for a particular time. Therefore, the selection of a particular delivery date by the short futures trader is less critical. While quasi-arbitrage helps to mitigate the risks associated with the reverse cash-and-carry trade, risks still remain, particularly the risks associated with the short trader's options.

11. Assume economic and political conditions are extremely turbulent. How would this affect the value of the seller's options on the T-bond futures contract? If they have any effect on price, would they cause the futures price to be higher or lower than it otherwise would be?

   Generally, options are more valuable the greater the price risk inherent in the underlying good. This is certainly true for the seller's options on the T-bond futures contract. To see this most clearly, we focus on the wildcard option. Exploitation of the wildcard option depends on a favorable price development on any position day between the close of futures trading and the end of the period to announce delivery at 8 p.m., Chicago time. If markets are turbulent, there is a greater chance that something useful will occur in that time window on some day in the delivery month. The greater value of the seller's options in this circumstance would cause the futures price to be lower than it otherwise would be.

12. Explain the difference between the wildcard option and the end-of-the- month option.

   The wildcard option is the seller's option to initiate the delivery sequence based on information generated between the close of futures trading and 8 p.m., Chicago time, the time by which the seller must initiate the delivery sequence for a given day. The settlement price determined at the close of trading is the price that will be used for computing the invoice amount. Trading of the T-bond futures contract ceases on the eighth to last business day of the expiration month, and the settlement price on that day is used to determine the invoice amount for all deliveries. Any contracts not closed by the end of the trading period must be fulfilled by delivery. Even though the short trader must make delivery in this circumstance, the short trader still possesses an end-of-the-month option. The short trader can choose which day to deliver and can choose which bond to deliver. The short trader will deliver late in the month if the rate of accrual on the bond planned for delivery exceeds the short-term financing rate at which the bond is carried.

Also, changing market conditions can change which bond will be cheapest- to-deliver, and the right to wait and choose a later delivery date has value to the short trader.

13. Some studies find that interest rate futures markets were not very efficient when they first began but that they became efficient after a few years. How can you explain this transition?

The growing efficiency of these markets seems to be due to a market seasoning or maturation process. When these contracts were first initiated, it appears that some of their nuances were not fully appreciated. In particular, the complete understanding of the importance of the seller's options seems to have emerged only slowly.

14. Assume you hold a T-bill that matures in 90 days, when the T-bill futures expires. Explain how you could transact to effectively lengthen the maturity of the bill.

Buy the T-bill futures that expires in 90 days. After this transaction, you will be long a spot 90-day bill, and you will hold (effectively) a spot position in a 90-day bill to begin in 90 days. The combination replicates a 180-day bill.

15. Assume that you will borrow on a short-term loan in six months, but you do not know whether you will be offered a fixed rate or a floating rate loan. Explain how you can use futures to convert a fixed to a floating rate loan and to convert a floating rate to a fixed rate loan.

For convenience, we assume that the loan will be a 90-day loan. If the loan is to be structured as a floating rate loan, you can convert it to a fixed rate loan by selling a short-term interest rate futures contract (Eurodollar or T-bill) that expires at the time the loan is to begin. The rate you must pay will depend on rates prevailing at the time of the loan. If rates have risen you must pay more than anticipated. However, if rates have risen, your short position in the futures will have generated a profit that will offset the higher interest you must pay on the loan.

   Now assume that you contract today for a fixed interest rate on the loan. If rates fall, you will be stuck paying a higher rate than the market rate that will prevail at the time the loan begins. To convert this fixed rate loan to a floating rate loan, buy an interest rate futures that expires at the time the loan is to begin. Then, if rates fall, you will profit on the futures position, and these profits will offset the higher than market rates you are forced to pay on your fixed rate loan.

16. You fear that the yield curve may change shape. Explain how this belief would affect your preference for a strip or a stack hedge.

If the yield curve is to change shape, rates on different futures expirations for the same interest rate futures contract may change by different amounts. In this case, it is important to structure the futures hedge so that the futures cash flows match the exposure of the underlying risk more closely. Thus, if the cash market exposure involves the same amount at regular intervals over the future, a strip hedge will be more effective against changing yield curve shapes.

17. A futures guru says that tailing a hedge is extremely important because it can change the desired number of contracts by 30 percent. Explain why the guru is nuts. How much can the tailing factor reasonably change the hedge ratio?

To tail a hedge, one simply reduces the computed hedge ratio by discounting it at the risk-free rate for the time of the hedge. For convenience, we assume that the untailed computed hedge ratio is 1.0. If the hedging period is one year, a 30 percent effect would require an interest rate of 43 percent, because $.7 = (1/1.43)$. If the hedging horizon is long, say a full two years, the interest rate would still have to be 19.52 percent to generate the 30 percent effect, because $(1.1952)^2 = 1/.7$. Thus, it seems extremely improbable that the tailing effect could be so large.

18. We have seen in Chapter 4 that regression-based hedging strategies are extremely popular. Explain their weaknesses for interest rate futures hedging.

First, regression-based hedging (the RGR Model) involves statistical estimation, so the technique requires a data set for both cash and futures prices. This data may sometimes be difficult to acquire, particularly for an attempt to hedge a new security. Second, the RGR Model does not explicitly consider the differences in the sensitivity of different bond prices to changes in interest rates, and this can be a very important factor. The regression approach does include the different price sensitivities indirectly, however, since their differential sensitivities will be reflected in the estimation of the hedge ratio. Third, any cash bond will have a predictable price movement over time, and the RGR Model does not consider this change in the cash bond's price explicitly. However, the sample data used to estimate the hedge ratio will reflect this feature to some extent. Fourth, the RGR hedge ratio is chosen to minimize the variability in the combined futures-cash position over the life of the hedge. Since the RGR hedge ratio depends crucially on the planned hedge length, one might reasonably prefer a hedging technique focusing on the wealth position of the hedge when the hedge ends. After all, the wealth change from the hedge depends on the gain or loss when the hedge is terminated, not on the variability of the cash-futures position over the life of the hedge.

19. You estimate that the cheapest-to-deliver bond on the T-bond futures contract has a duration of 6.5 years. You want to hedge your medium-term Treasury portfolio that has a duration of 4.0 years. Yields are 9.5 percent on the futures and on your portfolio. Your portfolio is worth $120,000,000, and the futures price is 98-04. Using the PS Model, how would you hedge?

    From the text, the PS hedge ratio is:

$$N = - \left(\frac{R_F \, P_i \, D_i}{R_i \, FP_F \, D_F} \right) \text{RV}$$

    For this problem, we are entitled to assume that RV = 1.0 since no other value is specified. Applying this equation to our data gives:

$$N = - \frac{.095 \, (\$120,000,000) \, (4.0)}{.095 \, (\$98,125) \, (6.5)} = -752.57$$

    Therefore, the PS hedge would require selling about 753 T-bond futures.

20. Explain the relationship between the Bank Immunization Case and hedging with the PS Model.

    Both bank immunization and the PS Model rely essentially on the concept of duration. A PS hedge finds the futures position to make the combined cash/futures position have a duration of zero. Similarly, in bank immunization with equal asset and liability amounts, the asset duration is set equal to the liability duration. For the combined balance sheet, the overall duration is effectively zero as well. Therefore, the two techniques are quite similar in approach, even if they use different instruments to achieve the risk reduction.

21. Compare and contrast the BP Model and the RGR Model for immunizing a bond portfolio.

    The BP Model essentially is an immunization model that is suitable for the bank immunization case. The BP hedge ratio is found empirically, but it is the hedge ratio that gives a price movement on the futures position that offsets the price movement on the cash position. As such, it is effectively reflecting the duration of the two instruments. (Notice that the BP Model does not really help with the planning period case, because it considers only the effect of a current change in rates, not a change over some hedging horizon.) The RGR Model does not really take duration into account in any direct fashion, so it is not oriented toward immunizing at all.

7
Stock Index Futures: Introduction

Answers to Questions and Problems

1. Distinguish between the MMI and the Dow Jones Industrial Average.

    The Dow Jones Industrial Average (DJIA) includes 30 stocks, while the MMI has only 20. Most of the stocks in the MMI are included in the DJIA. The method for computing the two indexes is the same. Prices of shares represented in the index are added, and the sum is divided by a special divisor. The divisor adjusts for stock splits, stock dividends, and substitutions of one stock for another in the index. When it first contemplated a stock index futures contract, the CBOT sought to trade a DJIA futures, but Dow Jones successfully sued to prevent the contract from being traded. The American Stock Exchange then developed the MMI, which closely tracks the DJIA, and licensed it to the CBOT. As a consequence, the two indexes are very similar.

2. Assume that the MMI stands at 340.00 and the current divisor is 0.8. One of the stocks in the index is priced at $100.00 and it splits 2:1. Based on this information, answer the following questions:
    a. What is the sum of the prices of all the shares in the index before the stock split?

    The equation for computing the index is:

    $$\text{Index} = \frac{\sum_{i=1}^{N} P_i}{\text{Divisor}}$$

    If the index value is 340.00 and the divisor is .8, the sum of the prices must be 340.00(.8) = $272.00.

    b. What is the value of the index after the split? Explain.

    After the split, the index value is still 340.00. The whole purpose of the divisor technique is to keep the index value unchanged for events such as stock splits.

    c. What is the sum of the prices of all the shares in the index after the split?

The stock that was $100 is now $50, so the sum of the share prices is now $222.00.

d. What is the divisor after the split?

With the new sum of share prices at $222.00, the divisor must be .6529 to maintain the index value at 340.00.

3. What is the main difference in the calculation of the MMI and the S&P 500 index? Explain.

The S&P 500 index gives a weight to each represented share that is proportional to the market value of the outstanding shares. The MMI simply adds the prices of all of the individual shares, so the MMI effectively weights each stock by its price level.

4. For the S&P 500 index, assume that the company with the highest market value has a 1 percent increase in stock prices. Also, assume that the company with the smallest market value has a 1 percent decrease in the price of its shares. Does the index change? If so, in what direction?

The index value increases. The share with the higher market value has a greater weight in the index than the share with the smallest market value. Therefore, the 1 percent increase on the high market value share more than offsets the 1 percent decrease on the low market value share.

5. Table 7.3 shows the correlations among the four indexes. Explain why the correlation between the NYSE Composite and the S&P 500 should be the highest of all correlations.

These two indexes have the highest degree of overlap. The S&P 500 accounts for about 80 percent of the entire market value of the NYSE Composite, so the similarity between the stocks represented in these indexes exceeds the similarity for any other pair.

6. The S&P 500 futures is scheduled to expire in half a year, and the interest rate for carrying stocks over that period is 11 percent. The expected dividend rate on the underlying stocks for the same period is 2 percent of the value of the stocks. (The 2 percent is the half-year rate, not an annual rate.) Ignoring the interest that it might be possible to earn on the dividend payments, find the fair value for the futures if the current value of the index is 315.00.

Assuming the half-year rate is .11/2, the fair value is:

Fair Value = 315.00(1.055 - .02) = 326.025

Assuming semiannual compounding, the interest factor would be 1.0536 and the fair value would be:

Fair Value = 315.00(1.0536 - .02) = 325.57

7. Consider a very simple index like the MMI, except assume that it has only two shares, A and B. The price of A is $100.00, and B trades for $75.00. The current index value is 175.00. The futures contract based on this index expires in three months, and the cost of carrying the stocks forward is .75 percent per month. This is also the interest rate that you can earn on invested funds. You expect Stock A to pay a $3 dividend in one month and Stock B to pay a $1 dividend in two months. Find the fair value of the futures. Assume monthly compounding.

$$\text{Fair value} = 175.00(1.0075)^3 - \$3(1.0075)^2 - \$1(1.0075) = 174.91$$

8. Using the same data as in Problem 7, now assume that the futures trades at 176.00. Explain how you would trade with this set of information. Show your transactions.

At 176.00, the futures is overpriced. Therefore, the trader should sell the futures, buy the stocks and carry them forward to expiration, investing the dividend payments as they are received. At expiration, the total cost incurred to carry the stocks forward is 174.91, and the trader receives 176.00 as cash settlement, for a profit of 1.09 index units. (This ignores interest on daily settlement flows.)

9. Using the same data as in Problem 7, now assume that the futures trades at 174.00. Explain how you would trade with this set of information. Show your transactions.

At 174.00 the futures is underpriced. Therefore, the trader should buy the futures and sell the stocks short, investing the proceeds. The trader will have to borrow to pay the dividends on the two shares. At expiration, the total outlays, counting interest, have been:

$$\$175.00(1.0075)^3 - \$3(1.0075)^2 - \$1(1.0075) = 174.91$$

With the convergence at expiration, the trader can buy the stocks for 174.00 and return them against the short sale. This gives a profit of $.91.

10. For a stock index and a stock index futures constructed like the MMI, assume that the dividend rate expected to be earned on the stocks in the index is the same as the cost of carrying the stocks forward. What should be the relationship between the cash and futures market prices? Explain.

The cash and futures prices should be the same. In essence, an investment in the index costs the interest rate to carry forward. This cost is offset by the proceeds from the dividends. If these are equal, the effective cost of carrying the stocks in the index forward is zero, and the cash and futures prices should then be the same.

11. Your portfolio is worth $100 million and has a beta of 1.08 measured against the S&P futures, which is priced at 350.00. Explain how you would hedge this portfolio, assuming that you wish to be fully hedged.

The hedge ratio is:

$$\left(\frac{V_P}{V_F}\right) \beta_P = \text{number of contracts}$$

With our data we have:

$$\left(\frac{\$100,000,000}{(350.00)\,(500)}\right) 1.08 = 617.14$$

The cash value of the futures contract is 500 times the index value of 350.00, or $175,000. Therefore, the complete hedge is to sell 617 contracts.

12. You have inherited $50 million, but the estate will not settle for six months and you will not actually receive the cash until that time. You find current stock values attractive and you plan to invest in the S&P 500 cash portfolio. Explain how you would hedge this anticipated investment using S&P 500 futures.

Buy S&P 500 index futures as a temporary substitute for actually investing the cash in the stock market. Probably the best strategy is to buy the contract that expires closest in time to the expected date for receiving the cash. If the S&P 500 index value is 300.00, then the dollar value of one contract will be $150,000 (300.00 × $500). Therefore, you should achieve a good hedge by purchasing about 333 ($50,000,000/$150,000) contracts.

8
Stock Index Futures: Refinements

Answers to Questions and Problems

1. Explain the market conditions that cause deviations from a computed fair value price and that give rise to no-arbitrage bounds.

    The villains are market imperfections, principally transaction costs. When trading is sufficiently costly, the futures price can deviate somewhat from fair value, and no market forces will arise to drive the futures price back to its fair value. The greater the costs of trading, the farther the futures price can stray from its theoretical fair value without arbitrage coming into play to restore the relationship. These trading costs include: the bid-asked spread and direct transaction costs such as brokerage commissions and taxes. Also, restrictions on the use of the proceeds from short sales can be important.

2. The No-Dividend Index consists only of stocks that pay no dividends. Assume that the two stocks in the index are priced at $100 and $48, and assume that the corresponding cash index value is 74.00. The cost of carrying stocks is 1 percent per month. What is the fair value of a futures contract on the index that expires in one year?

    $$\text{Fair Value} = 74.00(1.01)^{12} = 83.3851$$

3. Using the same facts as in Problem 2, assume that the round-trip transaction cost on a futures is $30. The contract size, we now assume, is for 1,000 shares of each stock. Trading stocks costs $.05 per share to buy and the same amount to sell. Based on this additional information, compute the no-arbi- trage bounds for the futures price.

    From the cash-and-carry transactions we would buy the stocks, carry them to expiration, and sell the futures. This strategy would cost:

Purchase and carry stock:	- $148,000(1.01)^{12} = - $166,770
Stock transaction cost:	+ 1,000(2)($.05) = - $100
Futures transaction cost:	- $30
Total Outlay:	- $166,900

    For this strategy to generate a profit, the futures must exceed 83.450 per contract. For the reverse cash-and-carry, we would sell the stocks, invest the proceeds, and buy the futures:

Sell stock; invest proceeds:	$148,000(1.01)^{12} = $166,770$
Stock transaction cost:	$1,000(2)($.05) = -100
Futures transaction cost:	-$30
Total Inflow:	-$166,640

For this strategy to generate a profit, the futures must be less than 83.320 per contract. The no-arbitrage bounds on the futures range from 83.320 to 83.450.

4. Using the facts in Problems 2 and 3, we now consider differential borrowing and lending costs. Assume that the 1 percent per month is the lending rate and assume that the borrowing rate is 1.5 percent per month. What are the no-arbitrage bounds on the futures price now?

From the cash-and-carry transactions we would buy the stocks, carry them to expiration, and sell the futures. Now the financing cost is 1.5 percent per month. This strategy would cost:

Purchase and carry stock:	$-$148,000(1.015)^{12} = -$176,951$
Stock transaction cost:	$+1,000(2)($.05) = -100
Futures transaction cost:	-$30
Total Outlay:	-$176,821

For this strategy to generate a profit, the futures must exceed 88.411 per contract. The reverse cash-and-carry strategy is unaffected because the lending rate is still 1 percent. Therefore, the no-arbitrage bounds on the futures range from 83.320 to 88.411.

5. Using the facts in Problems 2-4, assume now that the short seller receives the use of only half of the funds in the short sale. Find the no-arbitrage bounds.

The cash-and-carry transactions are the same as in Problem 4 so they give an upper no-arbitrage bound of 88.411. For the reverse cash-and-carry, we would sell the stocks, invest the proceeds, and buy the futures:

Sell stock; invest 50% of proceeds:	$+$74,000(1.01)^{12} = $83,385$
Stock transaction cost:	$-1,000(2)($.05) = -100
Futures transaction cost:	-$30
Recoup 50% of unused funds:	+$74,000
Total Inflow:	+$157,255

For this strategy to generate a profit, the futures must be less than 78.628 per contract. The no-arbitrage bounds on the futures range from 78.628 to 88.411.

6. Consider the trading of stocks in an index and trading futures based on the index. Explain how different transaction costs in the two markets might cause one market to reflect information more rapidly than the other.

    Let us assume that it is more costly to trade the individual stocks represented in the index than it is to trade the futures based on the index. (Once in a while we assume something consistent with reality.) Traders with information about the future direction of stock prices will want to exploit that information as cheaply as possible. Therefore, they will be likely to trade futures rather than the stocks in the index. Trading futures causes the futures price to adjust, and through arbitrage links, the stock price adjusts to the new futures price. In this scenario, the futures market reflects the new information before the stock market does.

7. For index arbitrage, explain how implementing the arbitrage through program trading helps to reduce execution risk.

    Execution risk is the risk that the actual trade price will not equal the anticipated trade price. The discrepancy arises largely from the delay between order entry and order execution. By using program trading, orders are conveyed to the floor more quickly and receive more rapid execution. (At least this is true in the absence of exchange-imposed delays on program trades.) Therefore, the use of program trading techniques should help to reduce execution risk.

8. Index arbitragers must consider the dividends that will be paid between the present and the futures expiration. Explain how overestimating the dividends that will be received could affect a cash-and-carry arbitrage strategy.

    Assume a trader estimates a dividend rate that is higher than the actual dividend rate that will be achieved. Further assume that the market as a whole correctly forecasts the dividend rate. For this investor, a strategy of cash-and-carry arbitrage will appear to be more attractive than it really is. This trader will be expecting to receive more dividends than will actually be forthcoming, so the trader will underestimate the net cost of carrying stocks forward. This overestimate could lead the trader to expect a profit from the trade that will evaporate when adjusted for the actual dividends that will be received.

9. Explain the difference between the beta in the Capital Asset Pricing Model and the beta one finds by regressing stock returns against returns on a stock index.

The beta of the CAPM is a theoretical entity. The CAPM beta is a measure based on the relationship between a particular security and an unobserved and probably unobservable market portfolio. The beta estimated by regressing stock returns against the returns on an index is an estimate of that ideal CAPM beta. Because the index fails to capture the true market portfolio, the actually estimated beta must fail to capture the true CAPM beta. Nonetheless, the estimated beta may be a useful approximation of the true CAPM beta.

10. Explain the difference between an ex-ante and an ex-post minimum risk hedge ratio.

The ex-ante minimum risk hedge ratio is estimated using historical data. In hedging practice, this estimated hedge ratio is applied to a future time period. Almost certainly the hedge ratio that would have minimized risk in the future period (the ex-post hedge ratio) will not equal the estimated ex-ante hedge ratio. However, the ex-post minimum risk hedge ratio can only be known after the fact. Therefore, we must expect some inaccuracy in estimating a hedge ratio ex-ante and comparing it with the ideal ex-post hedge ratio.

11. Assume you hold a well-diversified portfolio with a beta of 0.85. How would you trade futures to raise the beta of the portfolio?

Buy a stock index futures. In effect, this action levers up the initial investment in stocks, effectively raising the beta of the stock investment. In principle, this levering up can continue to give any level of beta a trader desires.

12. An index fund is a mutual fund that attempts to replicate the returns on a stock index, such as the S&P 500. Assume you are the manager of such a fund and that you are fully invested in stocks. Measured against the S&P 500 index, your portfolio has a beta of 1.0. How could you transform this portfolio into one with a zero beta without trading stocks?

Sell S&P 500 Index futures in an amount equal to the value of your stock portfolio. After this transaction you are effectively long the index (your stock holdings) and short the index by the same amount (your short position in the futures). As a result, you are effectively out of the stock market, and the beta of such a position must be zero.

13. You hold a portfolio consisting of only T-bills. Explain how to trade futures to create a portfolio that behaves like the S&P 500 stock index.

    Buy S&P 500 Index futures. You should buy an amount of futures that equals the value of funds invested in T-bills. The resulting portfolio will replicate a portfolio that is fully invested in the S&P 500.

14. In portfolio insurance using stock index futures, we noted that a trader sells additional futures as the value of the stocks falls. Explain why traders follow this practice.

    The goal of portfolio insurance is to keep the value of a portfolio from falling below a certain level or, alternatively expressed, to ensure that the return achieved on a portfolio over a given horizon achieves a certain minimum level. At the same time, portfolio insurance seeks to retain as much potential for beating that minimum return as is possible. The difference between the portfolio's current value and the value it must have to meet the minimum target we will call the *cushion*. If the portfolio has no cushion, the only way to ensure that the portfolio will achieve the target return, or the target value, is for the portfolio to be fully hedged.

    We now consider the trader's response if the portfolio value is above the minimum level, that is, if there is some cushion and stock prices fall. The drop in stock prices reduces the cushion, so the trader must move to a somewhat more conservative position. This requires hedging a greater portion of the portfolio, which the trader does by selling futures. Therefore, an initial drop in prices requires the selling of futures, and each subsequent drop in prices requires the sale of more futures.

9

Foreign Exchange Futures

Answers to Questions and Problems

1. The current spot exchange rate for the dollar against the Japanese yen is 146 yen per dollar. What is the corresponding U.S. dollar value of one yen?

    The dollar value per yen is simply the inverse of the yen per dollar rate:

    $$1/146 = \$.0068 \text{ per yen}$$

2. You hold the current editions of *The Wall Street Journal* and *The Financial Times*, the British answer to the WSJ. In the WSJ, you see that the dollar/pound 90-day forward exchange rate is $2.00 per pound. In *The Financial Times*, the pound 90-day dollar/pound rate is £.45 per U.S. dollar. Explain how you would trade to take advantage of these rates, assuming perfect markets.

    These rates are inconsistent because a rate of $2.00 per pound implies that the cost of one dollar should be £.50. Therefore, an arbitrage opportunity is available by trading as follows:

Geographical Arbitrage Transactions

t = 0	
In New York, using the WSJ rates, sell $2.00 for £1.00 90-days forward.	$0
In London, using *The Financial Times* rates, sell £1.00 for $2.22 90-days forward.	$0
	Total Cash Flow $0
t = 90	
In New York, fulfill the forward contract by delivering $2.00 and collecting £1.00.	- $2.00 + £1.00
In London, fulfill the forward contract by delivering £1.00 and collecting $2.22.	- £1.00 + $2.22
	Total Cash Flow + $.22

3.   In Problem 2, we assumed that markets are perfect. What are some practical impediments that might frustrate your arbitrage transactions in Problem 2?

Transaction costs would be the major impediment. Every trade of foreign exchange faces a bid-asked spread. In addition, there is likely to be some commission to be paid, either in the form of an outright commission or in the form of an implicit commission for maintaining a trading function. In addition, forward contracts sometimes require margin, and this would be an additional cost that the potential arbitrageur must bear.

4.   In the WSJ, you see that the spot value of the German mark is $.63 and the Swiss franc is worth $.72. What rate of exchange do these values imply for the Swiss franc and German mark? Express the value in terms of marks per franc.

The rate of $.63 per mark implies a value of the mark equal to DM 1.5873 per $. The rate of $.72 per franc implies a value of the franc equal to SF 1.3889 per $. Therefore, DM 1.5873 and SF 1.3889 are equivalent amounts, both equal to $1. As a consequence, the value of the DM per SF must equal 1.5873/1.3889 = 1.1429.

5.   Explain the difference between a pegged exchange rate system and a managed float.

In a pegged exchange rate system, the value of a pegged currency is fixed relative to another currency. For example, many Caribbean countries peg the value of their currency to the U.S. dollar. In a managed float, the value of the currency is allowed to fluctuate as market conditions require. This is the floating part of the policy. In a managed float, the central bank intervenes in the market to influence the value of the currency by buying or selling its own currency.

6.   Explain why covered interest arbitrage is just like our familiar cash-and- carry transactions from Chapter 3.

In a cash-and-carry transaction, a trader sells the futures and buys the underlying good. The trader carries the underlying good to the expiration of the futures, paying the carrying cost along the way, and delivers the good against the futures. In covered interest arbitrage, the transaction has a similar structure. The trader sells the futures and buys the foreign currency. The trader carries the foreign currency to the expiration of the futures, paying the carrying costs along the way, and delivers the good against the futures. The carrying cost for the foreign currency consists of two components. First, there is the financing cost in the home currency for the funds borrowed to buy the foreign currency. Second, the foreign currency that is carried forward to delivery against the futures earns interest. This interest on the foreign currency offsets the first component of the carrying cost.

7. For covered interest arbitrage, what is the cost-of-carry? Explain carefully.

    The cost-of-carry is the difference between the home currency interest rate and the foreign currency interest rate. For covered interest arbitrage, the trader borrows the home currency and pays the domestic interest rate for these funds. The trader uses these funds to buy the foreign currency in the spot market, and invests the foreign currency to earn the foreign interest rate. Therefore, the cost-of-carry is the domestic interest rate minus the foreign interest rate.

8. The spot value of the German mark is $.65, and the 90-day forward rate is $.64. If the U.S. dollar interest factor to cover this period is 2 percent, what is the German rate? What is the cost of carrying a German mark forward for this period?

    From the Interest Rate Parity Theorem, we know that $1 invested in the U.S. must earn the same rate as the $1 converted into a foreign currency, investing at the foreign rate and converting the proceeds back into dollars via a forward contract initiated at the outset of the transactions. For our data:

    $$\$1(1.02) = (\$1/\$.65)(1 + r_{DM})\$.64$$

    where r_{DM} = the German interest rate for this 90-day period. Therefore, $r_{DM} = .0359$. This is also the cost to carry a German mark forward for the 90 days.

9. The French franc is worth $.21 in the spot market. The French franc futures that expires in one year trades for $.22. The U.S. dollar interest rate for this period is 10 percent. What should the French franc interest rate be?

    $$1.10 = (1/.21)(1 + r_{FF}).22$$

    where r_{FF} = the French franc interest rate for this period. Thus, $r_{FF} = .05$.

10. Using the data in Problem 9, explain which country is expected to experience the higher inflation over the next year. If the expected inflation rate in the U.S. is 7 percent, what inflation rate for the French franc does this imply?

    The franc is expected to increase in value against the dollar from being worth $.21 now to $.22 in one year. Assuming PPP, this implies that the purchasing value of the dollar will decline relative to the franc.
    If the expected inflation rate in the U.S. is 7 percent, the real rate of interest is given by the equation:

    $$1.10 = (1.07)(1 + r^*)$$

where $r*$ is the real rate of interest in the U.S., and $r* = .028$. Assuming identical real rates in the U.S. and France, the expected French inflation rate is given by:

$$1.05 = [1 + E(I)](1.028)$$

where $E(I)$ is the expected inflation rate in France, and it equals $.0214$.

11. Using the data of Problem 9, assume that the French franc interest rate for the year is also 10 percent. Explain how you might transact faced with these values.

Faced with the exchange rates of Problem 9 and interest rates in both the U.S. and France of 10 percent, we could sell dollars for francs in the spot market, invest the franc proceeds at 10 percent, and arrange now to convert the franc funds in one year at the forward rate of $.22. Assuming an initial amount of $100, we would:

Dollar vs. Franc Arbitrage

$t = 0$

Borrow $100 for one year at 10%.	+ $100.00
Sell $100 for FF 476.19 in the spot market.	+ FF 476.19
	- $100.00
Invest FF 476.19 at 10% in France.	- FF 476.19
Sell FF 523.81 1 year forward for $115.24.	0

Total Cash Flow $0

$t = 1$ year

Collect FF 523.81 on investment.	+ FF 523.81
Deliver FF 523.81 on forward contract,	
collect $115.24.	- FF 523.81
	+ $115.24
Repay debt from borrowing $100.00.	- $110.00

Total Cash Flow + $5.24

12. Many travelers say that shoes in Italy are a big bargain. How can this be, given the Purchasing Power Parity Theorem?

Travelers are wrong as a matter of fact, but we still must answer the question. If PPP held with perfection, shoes would have the same cost in any currency and there would be no bargain shoes anywhere. Bargains can arise, however, due to market imperfections. First, transportation is costly. As a consequence, shoes in Italy could be cheaper than the same shoes in New York. The New York shoes must include the transportation cost. Second, even ignoring transportation costs, there are barriers to the free flow of shoes around the world. Governments impose tariffs and quotas, which can affect the price. Thus, if the U.S. protects its shoe industry by imposing tariffs or quotas on the Italian shoes, they can cost more in the U.S., thereby making shoes in Italy a bargain.

13. For the most part, the price of oil is denominated in dollars. Assume that you are a French firm that expects to import 420,000 barrels of crude oil in six months. What risks do you face in this transaction? Explain how you could transact to hedge the currency portion of those risks.

   Here we assume that the price of oil is denominated in dollars. Further, contracts traded on the NYMEX in oil are also denominated in dollars. Therefore, hedging on the NYMEX will not deal with the currency risk the French firm faces. However, the French firm can hedge the currency risk it faces by trading forwards for the French franc. To see how the French firm can control both its risk with respect to oil prices and foreign exchange consider the following data. We assume a futures delivery date in six months for the oil and for foreign exchange forward contracts. The futures price of oil is $30 barrel, and the six-month forward price of a French franc is $.20. With these prices, the French firm must expect a total outlay of $12.6 million for the oil, and a total franc outlay of FF 63 million. By trading oil futures and French franc forwards, it can lock in this French franc cost. Because the crude oil contract is for 1,000 barrels, the French firm should buy 420 contracts. This commits it to a total outlay of $12.6 million. The French firm then sells FF 63 million in the forward market for $12.6 dollars. These two transactions lock in a price of FF 63 million for the oil.

14. A financial comptroller for a U.S. firm is reviewing the earnings from a German subsidiary. This sub earns DM 1 million every year with exactitude, and it reinvests those earnings in its own German operations. This plan will continue. The earnings, however, are translated into U.S. dollars to prepare the U.S. parent's financial statements. Explain the nature of the foreign exchange risk from the point of view of the U.S. parent. Explain what steps you think the parent should take to hedge the risk that you have identified.

   This risk is entirely translation risk, because we assume that the funds stay strictly in Germany. If the firm enters the futures or forward market to hedge the dollar value of the DM 1 million, it undertakes a transaction risk to hedge a translation risk. In other words, the firm increases its economic risk to hedge a purely accounting risk. From an economic point of view, this hedge would not make sense.

10

The Options Market

Answers to Questions and Problems

1. State the difference between a call and a put option.

    Call and put options are the two fundamental kinds of exchange traded options. They differ in the rights and privileges that ownership conveys. The owner of a call option has the right to buy the good that underlies the option at a specified price, with this right lasting until a stated expiration date. The put owner has the right to sell the good that underlies the option at a specified price with this right lasting until a stated expiration date. Thus, owning a call gives the right to buy and owning a put gives the right to sell. Correlatively, the seller of a call receives a payment and must sell the underlying good at the option of the call owner. The seller of a put receives a payment and must buy the underlying good at the option of the put owner.

2. How does a trader initiate a long call position, and what rights and obligations does such a position involve?

    To initiate a long call position, a trader buys a call option. At the time of purchase, the trader must pay the price of the option, which the seller of the call collects. Upon purchase, the owner of a call has the right to purchase the underlying good at the specified call price with that right lasting until the stated expiration date. The owner of a call has no obligations, once he or she pays the purchase price.

3. Can buying an option, whether a put or a call, result in any obligations for the option owner? Explain.

    The owner of a call or put has already paid the purchase price. After buying the option, the owner has only rights and no obligations. The option owner may exercise the option, sell it, or allow it to expire worthless, but the option owner is not compelled to do anything.

4. Describe all of the benefits that are associated with taking a short position in an option.

   Taking a short position in an option involves selling an option. Upon the sale, the seller receives a cash payment. This is the only benefit associated with selling an option. After receiving payment for the option, the seller has only potential obligations, because the seller may be required to perform at the discretion of the option owner.

5. What is the difference between a short call and a long put position? Which has rights associated with it, and which involves obligations? Explain.

   The short call position is obtained when a trader sells a call option. The seller of a call may be required to surrender the underlying good in exchange for the payment stated in the option contract. The short call position has a maximum benefit equal to the price that the seller received to enter the short call position. The short call position is most favorable when the price of the underlying good remains below the exercise price. Then the seller of the call retains the full price of the option as profit. The higher the stock price above the exercise price, the worse for the call seller.

   In a long put position, the trader buys a put option. Owning the put gives the trader the right to sell the underlying good at the stated exercise price until the option expires. The put purchaser profits when the price of the underlying good falls below the exercise price. Then the owner of the put can require the put seller to buy the underlying good at the exercise price. When the underlying good has a price above the exercise price, the long put trader cannot exercise and loses the entire purchase price of the option.

   In contrasting the short call and the long put positions, we note that the short call trader has a maximum profit equal to the original sales price, and the long put trader has a maximum loss equal to the original sales price. For the long put position, there is the chance of a virtually unlimited profit as the stock price falls to zero. For the short call position, there is the chance of a theoretically unlimited loss, as the stock price rises toward infinity.

6. Consider the following information. A trader buys a call option for $5 that gives the right to purchase a share of stock for $100. In this situation, identify: the exercise price, the premium, and the striking price.

   The premium is the same as the option price and equals $5. The exercise price is the same as the striking price and equals $100.

7. Explain what happens to a short trader when the option he or she has sold expires worthless. What benefits and costs has the trader incurred?

   At the time of trading, the short trader of a put or call receives a payment. This is the only benefit the short trader receives from trading. If the option expires worthless, then the option was not exercised and the short trader attains the maximum possible profit. In selling an option, the short trader exposes himself or herself to the risk that the purchaser will exercise. For accepting this risk, the seller has received the option premium. If the option expires worthless, the short trader has escaped that risk.

8.   Explain why an organized options exchange needs a clearinghouse.

The clearinghouse guarantees the financial integrity of the market and oversees the performance of traders in the market. If there were no clearinghouse, each trader would have to be concerned with the financial integrity of his or her trading partner. Assuring that the opposite trading party will perform as promised is difficult and expensive. With a clearinghouse, each trader has an assurance that the opposite side of his or her transaction will be fulfilled. The clearinghouse guarantees it.

9.   What is the difference between an American and a European option?

A European option can be exercised only at expiration, while an American option can be exercised at any time prior to expiration. This difference implies that the American option must be at least as valuable as the European option.

10. Assume a trader does not want to continue holding an option position. Explain how this trader can fulfill his or her obligations, yet close out the option position.

The trader will be either long or short. If the trader is long, he or she can close the position by selling the exact same option. The option that will be sold must be on the same underlying good, have the same expiration, and the same striking price as the original option that is to be closed. If the trader were short initially, the trader would close the position by buying the identical option. In essence, the trader closes the position by trading to bring his or her net position back to zero. Again, making sure that all characteristics of the option match is an essential condition.

11
Option Payoffs and Option Strategies

Answers to Questions and Problems

1. Consider a call option with an exercise price of $80 and a cost of $5. Graph the profits and losses at expiration for various stock prices.

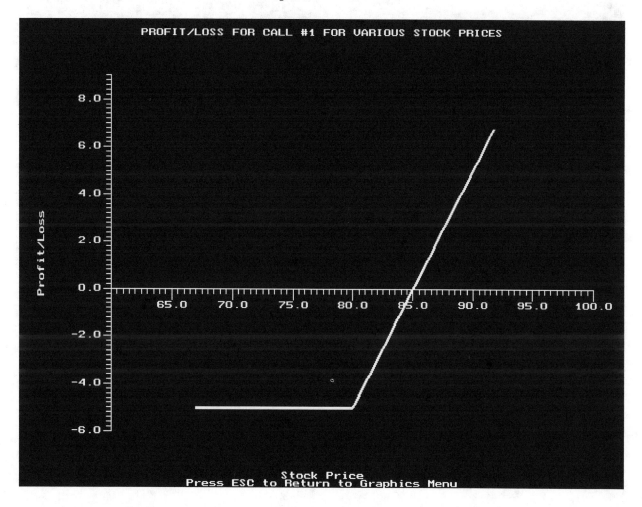

2. Consider a put option with an exercise price of $80 and a cost of $4. Graph the profits and losses at expiration for various stock prices.

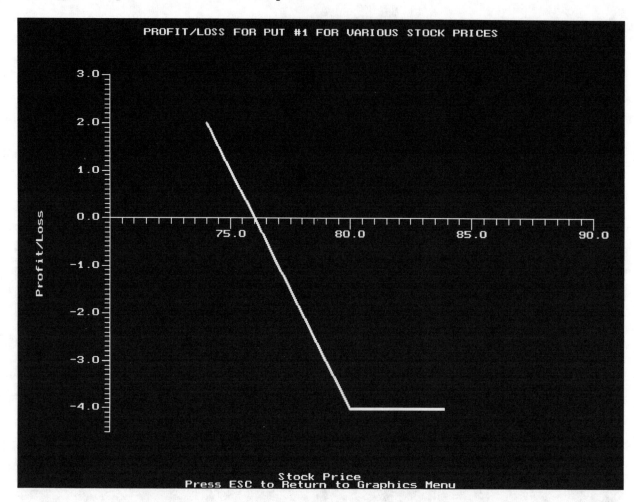

3. For the call and put in Questions 1 and 2, graph the profits and losses at expiration for a straddle comprising these two options. If the stock price is $80 at expiration, what will be the profit or loss? At what stock price (or prices) will the straddle have a zero profit?

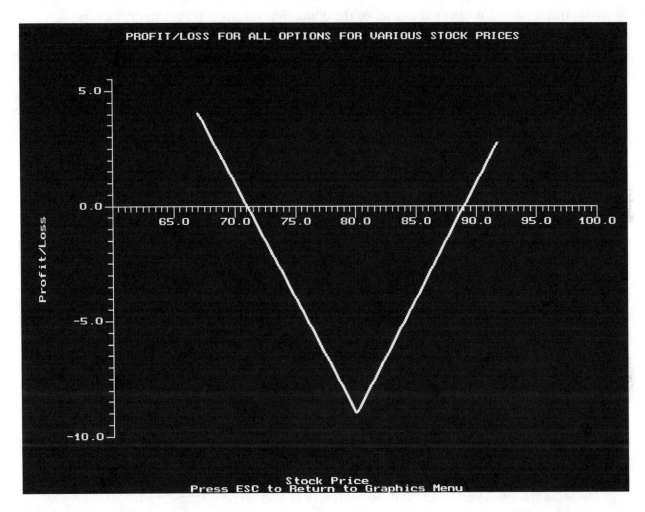

With a stock price at $80 at expiration, neither the call nor the put can be exercised. Both expire worthless, giving a total loss of $9. The straddle breaks even (has a zero profit) if the stock price is either $71 or $89.

4. A call option has an exercise price of $70 and is at expiration. The option cost $4 and the underlying stock trades for $75. Assuming a perfect market, how would you respond if the call is an American option? State exactly how you might transact. How does your answer differ if the option is European?

With these prices, an arbitrage opportunity exists because the call price does not equal the maximum of zero or the stock price minus the exercise price. To exploit this mispricing, one should buy the call and exercise it for a total out-of-pocket cost of $74. At the same time, the trader should sell the stock and deliver the stock just acquired through exercise for a $75 cash inflow. This produces a riskless profit without investment of $1. Because the option is at expiration, both the American and European options have the same right to exercise. Therefore, the American or European character of the option has no effect on the trading strategy.

5. A stock trades for $120. A put on this stock has an exercise price of $140 and is about to expire. The put trades for $22. How would you respond to this set of prices? Explain.

At expiration, the put price must equal the maximum of zero or the exercise price minus the stock price to avoid arbitrage. Therefore, the put price should be $20 in this situation, but it trades for $22. This difference gives rise to an arbitrage opportunity, because the put is priced too high relative to its theoretical value. To exploit this, the trader should simply sell the put and receive $22. Now the option can be exercised against the trader or not. If it is not exercised, the put expires worthless, the obligation is complete, and the trader retains the $22 as total profit. However, the purchaser of the option may choose to exercise immediately. In this case, the seller of the put must buy the stock for the exercise price of $140. The trader then sells the stock for $120 in the market, giving a $20 loss on the exercise. But the put seller already received $22, so he or she still has a $2 profit. In summary, selling the put leads to a $22 profit if the put buyer foolishly fails to exercise. Alternatively, if the put buyer exercises, the put seller still has a $2 profit. This is an arbitrage opportunity, because selling the overpriced put gives a profit without investment in all circumstances.

6. If the stock trades for $120 and the expiring put with an exercise price of $140 trades for $18, how would you trade?

As in the previous problem, these prices violate the no-arbitrage condition. Now, however, the put is underpriced relative to the other values. To conduct the arbitrage, the trader should buy the stock and buy and exercise the put. In this sequence of transactions, the trader pays $120 to acquire the stock, pays $18 to acquire the put, and receives $140 upon exercise of the put. These transactions yield a profit of $2 with no risk and no investment.

7. Consider a call and a put on the same underlying stock. The call has an exercise price of $100 and costs $20. The put has an exercise price of $90 and costs $12. Graph a short position in a strangle based on these two options. What is the worst outcome from selling the strangle? At what stock price or prices does the strangle have a zero profit?

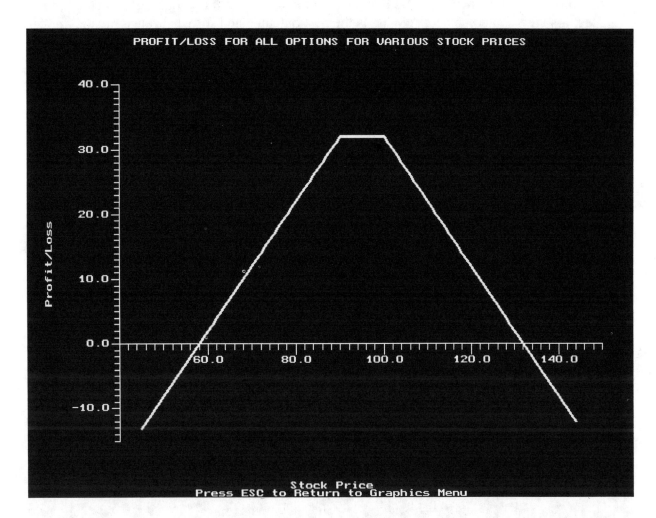

The worst outcomes occur when the stock price is very low or very high. First, the strangle loses $1 for each dollar the stock price falls below $58. With a zero stock price, the strangle loses $58. If the stock price is too high, the strangle also loses money. Because the stock could theoretically go to infinity, the potential loss on the strangle is unbounded. For stock prices of $58 or $132, the strangle gives exactly a zero profit.

8. Assume that you buy a call with an exercise price of $100 and a cost of $9. At the same time, you sell a call with an exercise price of $110 and a cost of $5. The two calls have the same underlying stock and the same expiration. What is this position called? Graph the profits and losses at expiration from this position. At what stock price or prices will the position show a zero profit? What is the worst loss that the position can incur? For what range of stock prices does this worst outcome occur? What is the best outcome and for what range of stock prices does it occur?

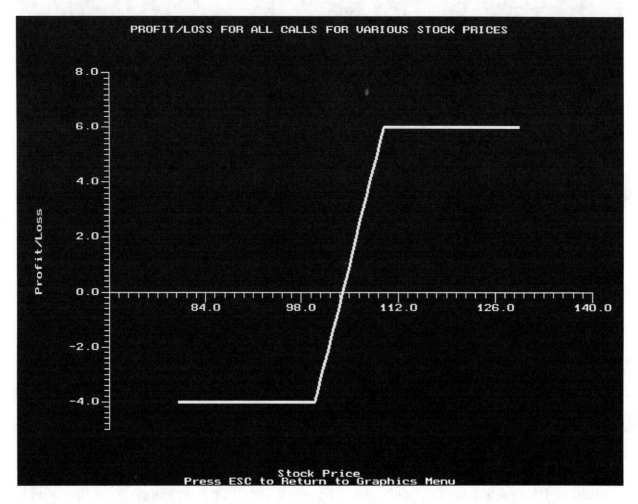

This position is a bull spread with calls, because it is designed to profit if the stock price rises. The entire position has a zero profit if the stock price is $104. At this point, the call with the $100 exercise price can be exercised for a $4 exercise profit. This $4 exercise value exactly offsets the price of the spread. The worst loss occurs when the stock price is $100 or below, because the option with the $100 exercise cannot be exercised, and the entire position is worthless. This gives a $4 loss. The best outcome occurs for any stock price of $110 or above and the total profit is $6.

9. Consider three call options with the same underlying stock and the same expiration. Assume that you take a long position in a call with an exercise price of $40 and a long position in a call with an exercise price of $30. At the same time, you sell two calls with an exercise price of $35. What position have you created? Graph the value of this position at expiration. What is the value of this position at expiration if the stock price is $90? What is the position's value for a stock price of $15? What is the lowest value the position can have at expiration? For what range of stock prices does this worst value occur?

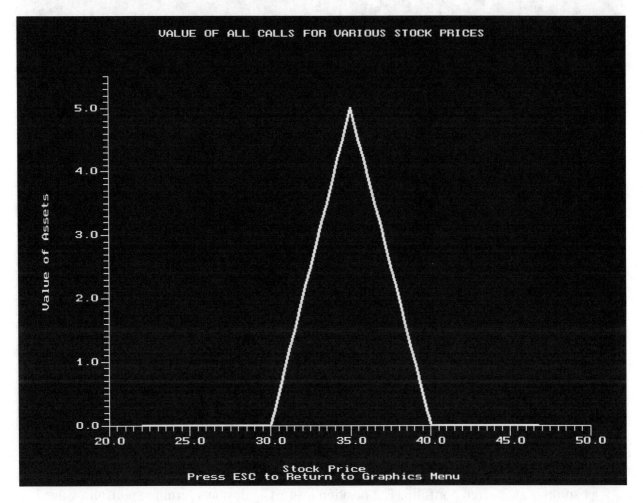

This is a long position in a butterfly spread. If the stock price is $90, the value of the spread is zero. For a $15 stock price, the spread is worth zero. The entire spread can be worth zero at expiration. This zero value occurs for any stock price of $30 or below and $40 or above.

10. Assume that you buy a portfolio of stocks with a portfolio price of $100. A put option on this portfolio has a striking price of $95 and costs $3. Graph the combined portfolio of the stock plus a long position in the put. What is the worst outcome that can occur at expiration? For what range of portfolio prices will this worst outcome occur? What is this position called?

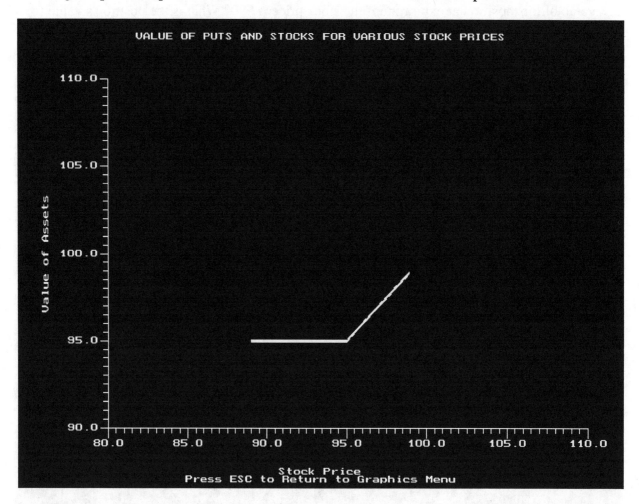

The worst result is a portfolio value of $95. The purchase of the put for $3 gives a loss of $8. This worst outcome occurs for a terminal stock portfolio value of $95 or less. This combined position is an insured portfolio. The position insures against any terminal portfolio value less than $95 or any loss greater than $8.

11. Consider a stock that sells for $95. A call on this stock has an exercise price of $95 and costs $5. A put on this stock also has an exercise price of $95 and costs $4. The call and the put have the same expiration. Graph the profit and losses at expiration from holding the long call and short put. How do these profits and losses compare with the value of the stock at expiration? If the stock price is $80 at expiration, what is the portfolio of options worth? If the stock price is $105, what is the portfolio of options worth? Explain why the stock and option portfolio differ as they do.

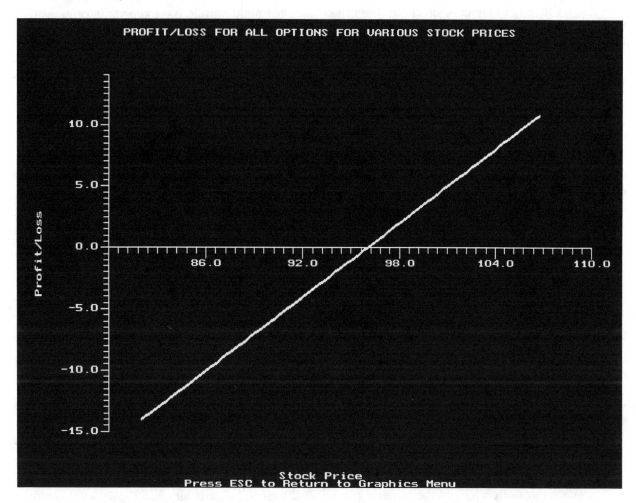

No matter what stock price results, the option portfolio will have $1 less profit than the stock itself. For example, the option portfolio costs $1, but both options are worthless at a stock price of $95. Therefore, at a stock price of $95, the stock has a zero profit, and the option portfolio has a $1 loss. Further, the option portfolio will be worth exactly $95 less than the stock at every price. With a stock price of $80, the call is worthless and the put will be exercised against the option holder for an exercise loss of $15. Therefore, the option portfolio is worth -$15 for an $80 stock price. If the stock trades for $105, the option portfolio will be worth $10.

12. Assume a stock trades for $120. A call on this stock has a striking price of $120 and costs $11. A put also has a striking price of $120 and costs $8. A risk-free bond promises to pay $120 at the expiration of the options in one year. What should the price of this bond be? Explain.

A portfolio consisting of one long call, one short put, and a riskless investment equal to the common exercise price of the two options gives exactly the same payoffs as a share of the underlying stock on the common expiration date. This put-call parity relationship requires that this portfolio of long call, short put, plus riskless investment should have the same price as the stock. With our data, the riskless bond must therefore cost $120 - $11 + $8 = $117. The riskless interest rate must be 2.53 percent.

13. In the preceding question, if we combine the two options and the bond, what will the value of this portfolio be relative to the stock price at expiration? Explain. What principle does this illustrate?

As the previous answer already indicated, the described portfolio (long call, short put, plus long bond) must have the same value as the stock itself. This illustrates the put-call parity relationship.

14. Consider a stock that is worth $50. A put and call on this stock have an exercise price of $50 and expire in one year. The call costs $5 and the put costs $4. A risk-free bond will pay $50 in one year and costs $45. How will you respond to these prices? State your transactions exactly. What principle do these prices violate?

These prices violate put-call parity. The long call, plus short put, plus riskless investment of the present value of the exercise price must together equal the stock price:

$$S = C - P + Xe^{-r(T-t)}$$

Instead, we have $50 \geq $5 - $4 + $45 = $46. Therefore, the stock is overpriced relative to the duplicating right-hand side portfolio. Accordingly, we transact as follows, with the cash flows being indicated in parentheses: Sell stock (+$50), buy call (-$5), sell put ($4), and buy the riskless bond (-$45). This gives a positive cash flow of $4 at the time of trading. To close our position, we collect $50 on the maturing bond. If the stock price is above $50, we exercise our call and use our $50 bond proceeds to acquire the stock, which we can then repay to close our short position. The put cannot be exercised against us, so we conclude the transaction with our original $4 profit. If the stock price is below $50, the put will be exercised against us. If so, we lose $50 - S on the exercise, paying our $50 bond proceeds to acquire the stock. Now with the stock in hand, we close our short position and the call expires worthless. As a result, we still have our $4 original cash inflow as profit. No matter what the stock price may be at expiration, our profit will be $4.

15. A stock sells for $80 and the risk-free rate of interest is 11 percent. A call and a put on this stock expire in one year and both options have an exercise price of $75. How would you trade to create a synthetic call option? If the put sells for $2, how much is the call option worth? (Assume annual compounding.)

    A synthetic call option consists of the following portfolio: long the stock, long the put, and short a risk-free bond paying the exercise price at the common maturity date of the call and put. Therefore, the following relationship must hold:

    $$C = S + P - \frac{X}{(1 + r)^t}$$

    Therefore, with the information given:

    $$C = \$80 + \$2 - \$67.67 = \$14.43$$

16. A stock costs $100 and a risk-free bond paying $110 in one year costs $100 as well. What can you say about the cost of a put and a call on this stock that both expire in one year and that both have an exercise price of $110? Explain.

    Put call parity implies:

    $$S - \frac{X}{(1 + r)^{T-t}} = C - P$$

    In this case, the stock and bond have the same price, so the left-hand side of the equation equals zero. For the right-hand side to equal zero, the call and put must have the same price as well. However, from the information given, we cannot determine what that price would be.

17. Assume that you buy a strangle with exercise prices on the constituent options of $75 and $80. You also sell a strangle with exercise prices of $70 and $85. Describe the payoffs on the position you have created. Does this portfolio of options have a payoff pattern similar to that of any of the combinations explored in this chapter?

    This position will profit for very low (say below $70) or very high (say above $85) stock prices at expiration. For prices in the range of $75 to $85, the position will lose. The exact breakeven points cannot be determined from the information given, however. In effect, the pair of strangles described is a short condor position.

18. If a stock sells for $75 and a call and put together cost $9 and the two options expire in one year and have an exercise price of $70, what is the current rate of interest?

    From the information given, and applying put-call parity, we know:

    $$S - \frac{X}{1+r} = C - P = \$9$$

    The stock price is $75 and must exceed the bond price by $9, so the price of the bond is $66. Thus, the present value of the $70 exercise price is $66, implying an interest rate of 6.06 percent.

19. Assume you buy a bull spread with puts that have exercise prices of $40 and $45. You also buy a bear spread with puts that have exercise prices of $45 and $50. What will this total position be worth if the stock price at expiration is $53? Does this position have any special name? Explain.

    The bull spread with puts and these exercise prices implies buying the put with $X = \$40$ and selling the put with $X = \$45$. To buy the bear spread implies buying a put with $X = \$50$ and selling a put with $X = \$45$. If the stock price at expiration is $53, all of the puts expire worthless. In making this trade, one has bought puts with $X = \$40$ and $X = \$50$, and sold two puts with $X = \$45$. This is equivalent to a long butterfly spread with puts.

20. Explain the difference between a box spread and a synthetic risk-free bond.

    The box spread gives a riskless payoff, so it is equivalent to a synthetic risk-free bond.

21. Within the context of the put-call parity relationship, consider the value of a call and a put option. What will the value of the put option be if the exercise price is zero? What will the value of the call option be in the same circumstance? What can you say about potential bounds on the value of the call and put option?

    If the exercise price of a put is zero, there can be no payoff from the put so the price must be zero. In this circumstance, the call must be worth the stock price. With respect to bounds on the option prices, the call price can never exceed the stock price and the put price can never exceed the exercise price.

22. Using the put-call parity relationship, write the value of a call option as a function of the stock price, the risk-free bond, and the put option. Now consider a stock price that is dramatically in excess of the exercise price. What happens to the value of the put as the stock price becomes extremely large relative to the exercise price? What happens to the value of the call option?

$$C = S + P - \frac{X}{(1 + r)^{T - t}}$$

The put price declines as the ratio S/X becomes large. The call option must increase in value. As we will see, the call must always be worth at least the stock price minus the present value of the exercise price.

12
Bounds on Option Prices

Answers to Questions and Problems

1. What is the maximum theoretical value for a call? Under what conditions does a call reach this maximum value? Explain.

    The highest price theoretically possible for a call option is to equal the value of the underlying stock. This happens only for a call option that has a zero exercise price and an infinite time until expiration. With such a call, the option can be instantaneously and costlessly exchanged for the stock at any time. Therefore, the call must have at least the value of the stock itself. Yet it cannot be worth more than the stock, because the option merely gives access to the stock itself. As a consequence, the call must have the same price as the stock.

2. What is the maximum theoretical value for an American put? When does it reach this maximum? Explain.

    The maximum value of a put equals the potential inflow of the exercise price minus the associated outflow of the stock price. The maximum value for this quantity occurs when the stock price is zero. At that time, the value of the put will equal the exercise price. In this situation, the put gives immediate potential access to the exercise price because it is an American option.

3. Answer Question 2 for a European put.

    As with the American put, the European put attains its maximum value when the stock price is zero. However, before expiration, the put cannot be exercised. Therefore, the maximum price for a European put is the present value of the exercise price, when the exercise price is discounted at the risk-free rate from expiration to the present. This discounting reflects the fact that the owner of a European put cannot exercise now and collect the exercise price. Instead, he or she must wait until the option expires.

4. Explain the difference in the theoretical maximum values for an American and a European put.

    The exercise value of a put option equals the exercise price (an inflow) minus the value of the stock at the time of exercise (an outflow). In our notation, this exercise value is $X - S$. For any put, the maximum value occurs when the stock is worthless, $S = 0$. The American and European puts have different maximum theoretical values because of the different rules governing early exercise. Because an American put can be exercised at any time, its maximum theoretical value equals the exercise price, X. If the stock price is zero at any time, an American put gives its owner immediate access to amount X through exercise. This is not true of a European put, which can be exercised only at expiration. If the option has time remaining until expiration and the stock is worthless, the European put holder must wait until expiration to exercise. With the stock worthless, the exercise will yield X to the European put holder. Because the exercise must wait until expiration, however, the put can be worth only the present value of the exercise price. Thus, the theoretical maximum value of a European put is $Xe^{-r(T-t)}$. In the special case of an option at expiration, $t = 0$, the maximum value for a European and an American put is X.

5. How does the exercise price affect the price of a call? Explain.

    The call price varies inversely with the exercise price. The exercise price is a potential liability that the call owner faces, because the call owner must pay the exercise price in order to exercise. The smaller this potential liability, other factors held constant, the greater will be the value of a call option.

6. Consider two calls with the same time to expiration that are written on the same underlying stock. Call 1 trades for $7 and has an exercise price of $100. Call 2 has an exercise price of $95. What is the maximum price that Call 2 can have? Explain.

    A no-arbitrage condition places an upper bound on the value of Call 2. The price of Call 2 cannot exceed the price of the option with the higher exercise price plus the $5 difference in the two exercise prices. Thus, the upper bound for the value of Call 2 is $12. If Call 2 is priced above $12, say, at $13, the following arbitrage becomes available.

    Sell Call 2 for cash flow +$13 and buy Call 1 for cash flow -$7. This is a net cash inflow of +$6. If Call 2 is exercised against you, you can immediately exercise Call 1. This provides the stock to meet the exercise of Call 1 against you. On the double exercise you receive $95 and pay $100, for a net cash flow of -$5. However, you received $6 at the time of trading for a net profit of $1. This is the worst case outcome.

    If Call 1 cannot be exercised, the profit is the full $6 original cash flow from the two trades. Also, if the stock price lies between $95 and $100 when Call 1 is exercised against you, it may be optimal to purchase the stock in the market rather than exercise Call 2 to secure the stock. For example, assume the stock trades for $98 when Call 1 is exercised against you. In this case, you buy the stock for $98 instead of exercising Call 2 and paying $100. Then your total cash flows are +$6 from the two trades, +$95 when Call 1 is exercised against you and -$98 from purchasing the stock to meet the exercise. Now your net arbitrage profit is $3. In summary, stock prices of $95 or below give a net profit of $6, because Call 1 cannot be exercised. Stock prices of $100 or above give a net profit of $1, because you will need to exercise Call 2 to meet the exercise of Call 1. Prices between $95 and $100 give a profit equal to +$6 +$95 - stock price at the time of exercise.

7. Six months remain until a call option expires. The stock price is $70 and the exercise price is $65. The option price is $5. What does this imply about the interest rate?

We know from the no arbitrage arguments that: $C \geq S - Xe^{-r(T-t)}$. In this case, we have $C = S - X$ exactly. Therefore, the interest rate must be zero.

8. Assume the interest rate is 12 percent and four months remain until an option expires. The exercise price of the option is $70 and the stock that underlies the option is worth $80. What is the minimum value the option can have based on the no-arbitrage conditions studied in this chapter? Explain.

We know from the no arbitrage arguments that: $C \geq S - Xe^{-r(T-t)}$. Substituting the specified values gives $C \geq \$80 - \$70e^{-.12(.33)} = \$80 - \$67.28 = \$12.72$. Therefore, the call price must equal or exceed $12.72 to avoid arbitrage.

9. Two call options are written on the same stock that trades for $70 and both calls have an exercise price of $85. Call 1 expires in six months and Call 2 expires in three months. Assume that Call 1 trades for $6 and that Call 2 trades for $7. Do these prices allow arbitrage? Explain. If they do permit arbitrage, explain the arbitrage transactions.

Here we have two calls that are identical except for their time to expiration. In this situation, the call with the longer time until expiration must have a price equal to or exceeding the price of the shorter-lived option. These values violate this condition, so arbitrage is possible as follows:

Sell Call 2 and buy Call 1 for a net cash inflow of $1. If Call 2 is exercised at any time, the trader can exercise Call 1 and meet the exercise obligation for a net zero cash flow. This retains the $1 profit no matter what happens. It may also occur that the profit exceeds $1. For example, assume that Call 2 cannot be exercised in the first three months and expires worthless. This leaves the trader with the $1 initial cash inflow plus a call option with a three month life, so the trader has an arbitrage profit of at least $1, perhaps much more.

10. Explain the circumstances that make early exercise of a call rational. Under what circumstances is early exercise of a call irrational?

Exercising a call before expiration discards the time value of the option. If the underlying stock pays a dividend, it can be rational to discard the time value to capture the dividend. If there is no dividend, it will always be irrational to exercise a call, because the trader can always sell the call in the market instead. Exercising a call on a no-dividend stock discards the time value, while selling the option in the market retains it. Thus, only the presence of a dividend can justify early exercise. Even in this case, the dividend must be large enough to warrant the sacrifice of the time value.

11. Consider a European and an American call with the same expiration and the same exercise price that are written on the same stock. What relationship must hold between their prices? Explain.

Because the American option gives every benefit that the European option does, the price of the American option must be at least as great as that of the European option. The right of early exercise inherent in the American option can give extra value if a dividend payment is possible before the common expiration date. Thus, if there is no dividend to consider, the two prices will be the same. If a dividend is possible before expiration, the price of the American call may exceed that of the European call.

12. Before exercise, what is the minimum value of an American put?

The minimum value of an American put must equal its value for immediate exercise, which is $X - S$. A lower price results in arbitrage. For example, assume $X = \$100$, $S = \$90$ and $P = \$8$. To exploit the arbitrage inherent in these prices, buy the put and exercise for a net cash outflow of -$98. Sell the stock for +$100 for an arbitrage profit of $2.

13. Before exercise, what is the minimum value of a European put?

For a put, the exercise value is $X - S$. However, a European put can be exercised only at expiration. Therefore, the present value of the exercise value is $Xe^{-r(T-t)} - S$, and this is the minimum price of a European put. For example, consider $X = \$100$, $S = \$90$, $T - t = .5$ years, and $r = .10$. The no-arbitrage condition implies the put should be worth at least $5.13.

Assume that the put actually trades for $5. With these prices, an arbitrageur could trade as follows. Borrow $95 at 10 percent for six months and buy the stock and the put. This gives an initial net zero cash flow. At expiration, the profit depends upon the price of the stock. First, there will be a debt to pay of $99.87 in all cases. If the stock price is $100 or above, the put is worthless and the profit equals $S - \$99.87$. Thus, the profit will be at least $.13, possibly much more. For stock prices below $100, exercise of the put yields $100, which is enough to pay the debt of $99.87 and keep $.13 profit.

14. Explain the differences in the minimum values of American and European puts before expiration.

The difference in minimum values for American and European puts stems from the restrictions on exercising a put. An American put offers the immediate access to the exercise value X if the put owner chooses to exercise. Because the European put cannot be exercised until expiration, the cash inflow associated with exercise must be discounted to $Xe^{-r(T-t)}$. The difference in minimum values equals the time value of the exercise price.

15. How does the price of an American put vary with time until expiration? Explain.

The value of an American put increases with the time until expiration. A longer-lived put offers every advantage that the shorter-lived put does. Therefore, a longer-lived put must be worth at least as much as the shorter-lived put. This implies that value increases with time until expiration. Violation of this condition leads to arbitrage.

16. What relationship holds between time until expiration and the price of a European put?

For a European put, the value may or may not increase with time until expiration. Upon exercise the put holder receives $X - S$. If the European put holder cannot exercise immediately, the inflow represented by the exercise price is deferred. For this reason, the value of a European put can be lower the longer the time until expiration. However, having a longer term until expiration also adds value to a put, because it allows more time for something beneficial to happen to the stock price. Thus, the net effect of time until expiration depends on these two opposing forces. Under some circumstances, the value of a European put will increase as time until expiration increases, but it will not always do so.

17. Consider two puts with the same term to expiration (six months). One put has a exercise price of $110, the other has an exercise price of $100. Assume the interest rate is 12 percent. What is the maximum price difference between the two puts if they are European? If they are American? Explain the difference, if any.

For two European puts, the price differential cannot exceed the difference in the present value of the exercise prices. With our data, the difference cannot exceed ($110 - $100)$e^{-.12(.5)}$ = $9.42. If the price differential on the European puts exceeds $9.42, we have an arbitrage opportunity. To capture the arbitrage profit, we sell the relatively overpriced put with the exercise price of $110 and buy the put with the $100 exercise price. If the put we sold is exercised against us, we accept the stock and dispose of it by exercising the put we bought. This will always guarantee a profit. For example, assume that the put with X = $100 trades for $5 and the put with X = $110 sells for $15, giving a $10 differential. We sell the put with X = $110 and buy the put with X = $100, for a net inflow of $10. We invest this until expiration, at which time it will be worth 10e^{.12(.5)}$ = $10.62. If the put we sold is exercised against us, we pay $110 and receive the stock. We can then exercise our put to dispose of the stock and receive $10. This gives a $10 loss on the double exercise. However, our maturing bond is worth $10.62, so we still have a profit of $.62.

For two American puts, the price differential cannot exceed the difference in the exercise prices. If it does, we conduct the same arbitrage. However, we do not have to worry about the discounted value of the differential, because the American puts carry the opportunity to exercise immediately and to gain access to the value of the mispricing at any time, not just at expiration.

18. How does the price of a call vary with interest rates? Explain.

For a call, the price increases with interest rates. The easiest way to see this is to consider the no-arbitrage condition: $C \geq S - Xe^{-r(T-t)}$. The higher the interest rate, the smaller will be the present value of the exercise price, a potential liability. With extremely high interest rates, the exercise price will have an insignificant present value and the call price will approach the stock price.

19. Explain how a put price varies with interest rates. Does the relationship vary for European and American puts? Explain.

Put prices vary inversely with interest rates. This holds true for both American and European puts. For the put owner, the exercise price is a potential inflow. The present value of this inflow, and the market value of the put, increases as the interest rate falls. Therefore, put prices rise as interest rates fall.

20. What is the relationship between the risk of the underlying stock and the call price? Explain in intuitive terms.

Call prices rise as the riskiness of the underlying stock increases. A call option embodies insurance against extremely bad outcomes. Insurance is more valuable the greater the risk it insures against. Therefore, if the underlying stock is very risky, the insurance embedded in the call is more valuable. As a consequence, call prices vary directly with the risk of the underlying good.

21. A stock is priced at $50 and the risk-free rate of interest is 10 percent. A European call and a European put on this stock both have exercise prices of $40 and expire in six months. What is the difference between the call and put prices? (Assume continuous compounding.) From the information supplied in this question, can you say what the call and put prices must be? If not, explain what information is lacking.

From put-call parity, $S - Xe^{-r(T-t)} = C - P$. Therefore, the $C - P$ must equal:

$$\$50 - \$40e^{-.5(.1)} = \$11.95$$

We cannot determine what the two option prices are. Information about how the stock price might move is lacking.

22. A stock is priced at $50 and the risk-free rate of interest is 10 percent. A European call and a European put on this stock both have exercise prices of $40 and expire in six months. Assume that the call price exceeds the put price by $7. Does this represent an arbitrage opportunity? If so, explain why and state the transactions you would make to take advantage of the pricing discrepancy.

From Question 21, we saw that the call price must exceed the put price by $11.95 according to put-call parity. Therefore, if the difference is only $7, there is an arbitrage opportunity, and the call price is cheap relative to the put. The long call/short put position is supposed to be worth the same as the long stock/short bond position. But the long call/short put portfolio costs only $7, not the theoretically required $11.95. To perform the arbitrage we would buy the relatively underpriced portfolio and sell the relatively overpriced portfolio. Specifically we would: buy the call, sell the put, sell the stock, and buy the risk-free bond that pays the exercise price in six months. From these transactions we would have the following cash flows: from buying the call and selling the put -$7; from selling the stock +$50, and from buying the risk-free bond -$38.05, for a net cash flow of $4.95. This net cash flow exactly equals the pricing discrepancy.

At expiration, we can fulfill all of our obligations with no further cash flows. If the stock price is below the exercise price, the put we sold will be exercised against us and we must pay $40 and receive the stock. We will have the $40 from the maturing bond, and we use the stock that we receive to repay our short sale on the stock. If the stock price exceeds $40, we exercise our call and use the $40 proceeds to pay the exercise price. We then fulfill our short sale by returning the share.

13
European Option Pricing

Answers to Questions and Problems

1. What is binomial about the binomial model? In other words, how does the model get its name?

    The binomial model is binomial because it allows for two possible stock price movements. The stock can either rise by a certain amount or fall by a certain amount. No other stock price movement is possible.

2. If a stock price moves in a manner consistent with the binomial model, what is the chance that the stock price will be the same for two periods in a row? Explain.

    There is no chance. In every period, the stock price will either rise or fall. Therefore, in two adjacent periods, the stock price cannot be the same. From this period to the next, the stock price must necessarily rise or fall. However, the stock price can later return to its present price. This depends on the up and down factors for the change in the stock price.

3. Assume a stock price is $120 and in the next year it will either rise by 10 percent or fall by 20 percent. The risk-free interest rate is 6 percent. A call option on this stock has an exercise price of $130. What is the price of a call option that expires in one year? What is the chance that the stock price will rise?

    Our data are:

$$C_u = \$2$$

$$C_d = \$0$$

$$US = \$132$$

$$DS = \$96$$

$$R = 1.06$$

$$B^* = \frac{(C_u D - C_d U)}{[(U - D)R]} = \frac{2(0.8) - 0(1.1)}{(1.1 - 0.8)(1.06)} = \$5.03$$

$$N^* = \frac{C_u - C_d}{(U - D)S} = \frac{2 - 0}{(1.1 - 0.8)120} = 0.0556$$

Therefore, $C = .0556(\$120) - \$5.03 = \$1.64$. The probability of a stock price increase is:

$$(R - D)/(U - D) = (1.06 - .8)/(1.1 - .8) = .8667$$

4. Based on the data in Question 3, what would you hold to form a risk-free portfolio?

Because $C = N^*S - B^*$, the portfolio of $C - N^*S + B^*$ should be a riskless portfolio.

5. Based on the data in Question 3, what will the price of the call option be if the option expires in two years and the stock price can move up 10 percent or down 20 percent in each year?

Terminal stock prices in two periods are given as follows: $UUS = \$145.20$, $DDS = \$76.80$, and $UDS = DUS = \$105.60$. The probabilities of these different terminal stock prices are: $\pi_{uu} = (.8667)(.8667) = .7512$, $\pi_{ud} = (.8667)(.1333) = .1155$, $\pi_{du} = (.1333)(.8667) = .1155$, and $\pi_{dd} = (.1333)(.1333) = .0178$. The call price at expiration equals the terminal stock price minus the exercise price of $100, or zero, whichever is larger. Therefore, we have $C_{uu} = \$15.20$, $C_{dd} = 0$, $C_{du} = C_{ud} = 0$.

   We have already found that the probability of an increase is .8667, so the probability of a down movement is .1333. Because the option pays off only with two increases, we need consider only that path. Thus, the value of the call is:

$$C = \pi_{uu}C_{uu}/R^2 = (.7512)(\$15.20)/(1.06)^2 = \$10.16$$

6. Based on the data in Question 3, what would the price of a call with one year to expiration be if the call has an exercise price of $135? Can you answer this question without making the full calculations? Explain.

    From Question 3, we see that US = $132. This is not enough to bring the call into the money. Therefore, we know that the call must expire worthless, so its current price is zero.

7. A stock is worth $60 dollars today. In a year, the stock price can rise or fall by 15 percent. If the interest rate is 6 percent, what is the price of a call option that expires in three years and has an exercise price of $70? What is the price of a put option that expires in three years and has an exercise price of $65? (Use **OPTION!** to solve this problem.)

    The call is worth $6.12 and the put is worth $3.04. The two trees from **OPTION!** are shown on the following page:

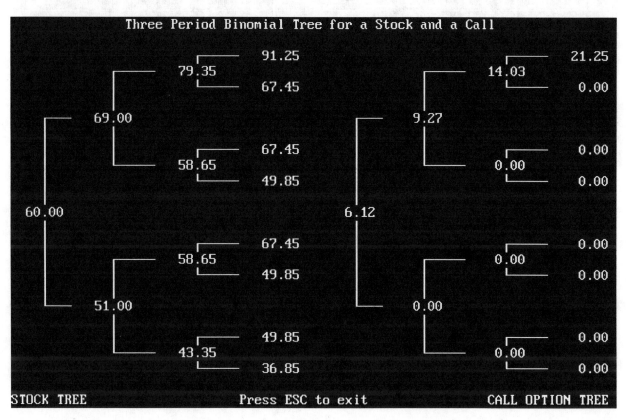

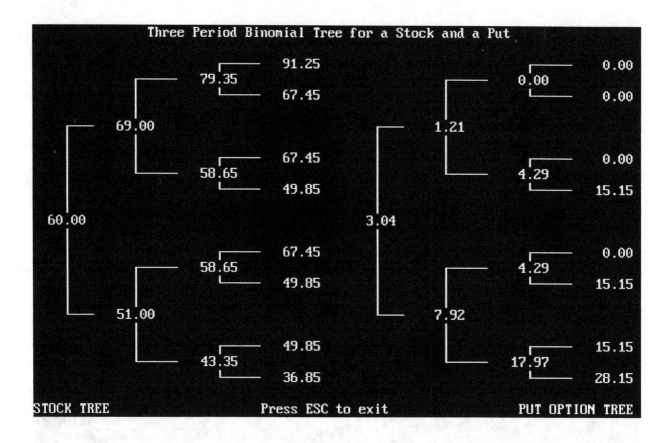

Three Period Binomial Tree for a Stock and a Put

STOCK TREE   Press ESC to exit   PUT OPTION TREE

8. Consider our model of stock price movements given in Equation 13.8. A stock has an initial price of $55 and an expected growth rate of .15 per year. The annualized standard deviation of the stock's return is .4. What is the expected stock price after 175 days?

Substituting values for our problem, and realizing that the expected value of a drawing for a $N(0,1)$ distribution is zero, gives:

$$S_{t+1} - S_{-t} = \$55(.15)(175/365) = \$3.96$$

Adding this amount to the initial stock price of $55 gives $58.96 as the expected stock price in 175 days.

9. A stock sells for $110. A call option on the stock has an exercise price of $105 and expires in 43 days. If the interest rate is .11 and the standard deviation of the stock's returns is .25, what is the price of the call according to the Black-Scholes model? What would be the price of a put with an exercise price of $140 and the same time until expiration?

$$d_1 = \frac{\ln\left[\frac{110}{105}\right] + [.11 + .5(.25)(.25)]\left[\frac{43}{365}\right]}{.25\sqrt{\frac{43}{365}}} = .7361$$

$$d_2 = d_1 - \sigma\sqrt{t} = .7361 - .25\sqrt{\frac{43}{365}} = .6503$$

From the **OPTION!** software, $N(.7361) = .769165$ and $N(.6503) = .742251$. Therefore,

$$c = \$110(.769165) - \$105e^{-.11(43/365)}(.742251) = \$7.6752.$$

For the put option with $X = \$140$:

$$d_1 = \frac{\ln\left[\frac{110}{140}\right] + [.11 + .5(.25)(.25)]\left[\frac{43}{365}\right]}{.25\sqrt{\frac{43}{365}}} = -2.6177$$

$$d_2 = d_1 - \sigma\sqrt{t} = -2.6177 - .25\sqrt{\frac{43}{365}} = -2.7035$$

The Black-Scholes put pricing model is:

$$p_t = Xe^{-r(T-t)}N(-d_2) - S_tN(-d_1)$$

$N(2.7035) = .996569$ and $N(2.6177) = .995574$. Therefore,

$$p_t = \$140e^{-.11(43/365)}(.996569) - \$110(.995574) = \$28.21$$

10. Consider a stock that trades for $75. A put and a call on this stock both have an exercise price of $70 and they expire in 150 days. If the risk-free rate is 9 percent and the standard deviation for the stock is .35, compute the price of the options according to the Black-Scholes model.

$$d_1 = \frac{\ln\left[\dfrac{75}{70}\right] + [.09 + .5(.35)(.35)]\left[\dfrac{150}{365}\right]}{.35\sqrt{\dfrac{150}{365}}} = .5845$$

$$d_2 = d_1 - \sigma\sqrt{t} = .5845 - .35\sqrt{\dfrac{150}{365}} = .3601$$

$N(.5845) = .720558$, $N(.3601) = .640614$, $N(-.5845) = .279442$, $N(-.3601) = .359386$.

$$c_t = \$75(.720558) - \$70\,e^{-.09(150/365)}\,(.640614) = \$54.04 - \$43.21 = \$10.83$$

$$p_t = \$70e^{-.09(150/365)}\,(.359386) - \$75\,(.279442) = \$24.24 - \$20.96 = \$3.29$$

11. For the options in Question 10, now assume that the stock pays a continuous dividend of 4 percent. What are the options worth according to Merton's model?

$$d_1^M = \frac{\ln\left[\dfrac{75}{70}\right] + [.09 - .04 + .5(.35)(.35)]\left[\dfrac{150}{365}\right]}{.35\sqrt{\dfrac{150}{365}}} = .5113$$

$$d_2^M = d_1^M - \sigma\sqrt{t} = .5113 - .35\sqrt{\dfrac{150}{365}} = .2869$$

$N(.5113) = .695430$; $N(.2869) = .304570$; $N(-.5113) = .612906$; and $N(-.2869) = .387094$.

$$c_t^M = e^{-.04(150/365)}\,\$75\,(.695430) - \$70\,e^{-.09(150/365)}\,(.612906) = \$9.96$$

$$p_t^M = \$70\,e^{-.09(150/365)}\,(.387094) - \$75\,e^{-.04(150/365)}\,(.304570) = \$3.64$$

12. Consider a Treasury bill with 173 days until maturity. The bid and asked yields on the bill are 9.43 and 9.37. What is the price of the T-bill? What is the continuously compounded rate on the bill?

From the text, we have:

$$P_{TB} = 1 - .01 \left(\frac{B + A}{2} \right) \left(\frac{\text{Days Until Maturity}}{360} \right)$$

$$= 1 - .01 \left(\frac{9.43 + 9.37}{2} \right) \left(\frac{173}{360} \right)$$

$$= .9548$$

Therefore, the price of the bill is 95.48 percent of par. To find the corresponding continuously compounded rate, we solve the following equation for r:

$$e^{r(T - t)} = 1/PTB$$

$$e^{r\,(173/365)} = 1/.9548$$

$$r = .0962$$

Thus, the continuously compounded rate on the bill is 9.62 percent.

13. Consider the following sequence of daily stock prices: $47, $49, $46, $45, $51. Compute the mean daily logarithmic return for this share. What is the daily standard deviation of returns? What is the annualized standard deviation?

Let P_t = the price on day t, $PR_t = P_t/P_{t-1}$, PR_μ = the mean daily logarithmic return, and σ = the standard deviation of the daily logarithmic return. Then,

PR_t	$\ln(PR_t)$	$[\ln PR_t - PR_\mu]^2$
1.0426	.0417	.000454
.9388	-.0632	.006989
.9783	-.0219	.001789
1.1333	.1251	.010962

$$PR_\mu = (.0417 - .0632 - .0219 + .1251)/4 = .0204$$

$$\text{VAR}(PR) = (1/3)(.000454+.006989+.001789+.010962) = .006731.$$

σ = the square root of .006731 = .082045.

The annualized $\sigma = \sigma$ times the square root of 250 = 1.2972.

14. A stock sells for $85. A call option with an exercise price of $80 expires in 53 days and sells for $8. The risk-free interest rate is 11 percent. What is the implied standard deviation for the stock? (Use **OPTION!** to solve this problem.)

$\sigma = .332383$. It is also possible to find this value by repeated application of the Black-Scholes formula. For example, with this option data, different trial values of σ give the following sequence of prices:

Call Price:	Trial Value of σ:	σ is:
$6.29	.1	too low
9.84	.5	too high
7.67	.3	too low
8.72	.4	too high
8.18	.35	too high
7.98	.33	too low
8.03	.335	too high
8.01	.333	too high
8.00	.332	very close

The **OPTION!** program follows a search like this to zero in on the correct value of σ so that the resulting option price matches the actual price.

15. For a particular application of the binomial model, assume that $U = 1.09$, $D = .91$, and that the two are equally probable. Do these assumptions lead to any particular difficulty? Explain. (Note: These are specified up and down movements and are not intended to be consistent with the Black-Scholes model.)

    Note that $.5 (1.09) + .5 (.91) = 1.0$, so the expected return on the stock is zero. The expected return on the stock must equal the risk-free rate in the risk neutral setting of the binomial model. Therefore, these up and down factors imply a zero interest rate.

16. For a stock that trades at $120 and has a standard deviation of returns of .4, use the Black-Scholes model to price a call and a put that expire in 180 days and that have an exercise price of $100. The risk-free rate is 8 percent. Now assume that the stock will pay a dividend of $3 on day 75. Apply the known dividend adjustment to the Black-Scholes model and compute new call and put prices.

    With no dividends, the call price is $27.54, and the put price is $3.67. With the known dividend adjustment, the call price is $25.14, and the put price is $4.23.

17. A call and a put expire in 150 days and have an exercise price of $100. The underlying stock is worth $95 and has a standard deviation of .25. The risk-free rate is 11 percent. Use a three-period binomial model and stock price movements consistent with the Black-Scholes model to compute the value of these options. Specify U, D, and π_u, as well as the values for the call and put.

    The call price is $5.80, and the put price is $6.38. $U = 1.0969$, and $D = .9116$.

    $$\pi_U = \frac{e^{.11\left[\frac{50}{365}\right]} - .9116}{1.0969 - .9116} = .5590$$

18. For the situation in Problem 17, assume that the stock will pay 2 percent of its value as a dividend on day 80. Compute the value of the call and the put under this circumstance.

    Recalling that these are European options, the call is worth $4.66, and the put is worth $7.14.

19. For the situation in Problem 17, assume that the stock will pay a dividend of $2 on day 80. Compute the value of the call and the put under this circumstance.

    The call is worth $4.62, and the put is worth $7.16.

20. Consider the first tree in Figures 13.10 and 13.12. If the stock price falls in both of the first two periods, the price is $65.59. For the first tree in Figure 13.12, the put value is $8.84 in this case. Given that the exercise price on the put is $75, does this present a contradiction? Explain.

    The apparent contradiction arises because the intrinsic value of the put is $75 - $65.59 = $9.41, which exceeds the put price of $8.84. However, because this is a European put, it cannot be exercised to capture the intrinsic value prior to expiration. Thus, the European put price can be less than the intrinsic value.

21. Consider the second tree in Figures 13.10 and 13.11. If the stock price increases in the first period, the price is $88.35. For the second tree in Figure 13.11, the call price is $12.94 in this case. Given that the exercise price on the put is $75, does this present a contradiction? Explain.

    One of the arbitrage conditions we have considered says that the call price must equal or exceed $S - X$. In this situation, $S - X = \$88.35 - \$75.00 = \$13.35$, which is greater than the call price of $12.94. Thus, it appears that an arbitrage opportunity exists. The apparent contradiction dissolves when we realize that the call price reflects the dividend that will occur before the option can be exercised.

14

Option Sensitivities and Option Hedging

Answers to Questions and Problems

1. Consider Call A, with: $X = \$70$; $r = .06$; $T - t = 90$ days; $\sigma = .4$; and $S = \$60$. Compute the price, DELTA, GAMMA, THETA, VEGA, and RHO for this call.

$$c = \$1.82$$
$$DELTA = .2735$$
$$GAMMA = .0279$$
$$THETA = -8.9173$$
$$VEGA = 9.9144$$
$$RHO = 3.5985$$

2. Consider Put A, with: $X = \$70$; $r = .06$; $T - t = 90$ days; $\sigma = .4$; and $S = \$60$. Compute the price, DELTA, GAMMA, THETA, VEGA, and RHO for this put.

$$p = \$10.79$$
$$DELTA = -.7265$$
$$GAMMA = .0279$$
$$THETA = -4.7790$$
$$VEGA = 9.9144$$
$$RHO = -13.4083$$

3. Consider a straddle comprised of Call A and Put A. Compute the price, DELTA, GAMMA, THETA, VEGA, and RHO for this straddle.

$$
\begin{aligned}
\text{price} = c + p \quad &= \quad \$12.61 \\
\text{DELTA} \quad &= \quad .2735 - .7265 = -.4530 \\
\text{GAMMA} \quad &= \quad .0279 + .0279 = .0558 \\
\text{THETA} \quad &= \quad -8.9173 - 4.47790 = -13.6963 \\
\text{VEGA} \quad &= \quad 9.9144 + 9.9144 = 19.8288 \\
\text{RHO} \quad &= \quad 3.5985 - 13.4083 = -9.8098
\end{aligned}
$$

4. Consider Call A. Assuming the current stock price is $60, create a DELTA-neutral portfolio consisting of a short position of one call and the necessary number of shares. What is the value of this portfolio for a sudden change in the stock price to $55 or $65?

   As we saw for this call, DELTA = .2735. The DELTA-neutral portfolio, given a short call component is .2735 shares - 1 call, costs:

$$.2735 \, (\$60) - \$1.82 = \$14.59$$

   If the stock price goes to $55, the call price is $.77, and the portfolio will be worth:

$$.2735 \, (\$55) - \$.77 = \$14.27$$

   With a stock price of $65, the call is worth $3.55, and the portfolio value is:

$$.2735 \, (\$65) - \$3.55 = \$14.23$$

   Notice that the portfolio values are lower for both stock prices of $55 and $65, reflecting the negative GAMMA of the portfolio.

5. Consider Call A and Put A from above. Assume that you create a portfolio that is short one call and long one put. What is the DELTA of this portfolio? Can you find the DELTA without computing? Explain. Assume that a share of stock is added to the short call/long put portfolio. What is the DELTA of the entire position?

   The DELTA of the portfolio is -1.0 = -.2735 - .7265. This is necessarily true, because the DELTA of the call is $N(d_1)$, the DELTA of the put is $N(-d_2)$, and $N(d_1) + N(d_2) = 1.0$. If a long share of stock is added to the portfolio, the DELTA will be zero, because the DELTA of a share is always 1.0.

6. What is the GAMMA of a share of stock if the stock price is $55 and a call on the stock with $X = \$50$ has a price $c = \$7$ while a put with $X = \$50$ has a price $p = \$4$? Explain.

    The GAMMA of a share of stock is always zero. All other information in the question is irrelevant. The GAMMA of a share is always zero because the DELTA of a share is always 1.0. As GAMMA measures how DELTA changes, there is nothing to measure for a stock since the DELTA is always 1.0.

7. Consider Call B written on the same stock as Call A with: $X = \$50$; $r = .06$; $T - t = 90$ days; $\sigma = .4$; and $S = \$60$. Form a bull spread with calls from these two instruments. What is the price of the spread? What is its DELTA? What will the price of the spread be at expiration if the terminal stock price is $60? From this information, can you tell whether THETA is positive or negative for the spread? Explain.

    As observed in Problem 1, for Call A, $c = \$1.82$, DELTA = .2735, and THETA = -8.9173. For Call B, c = \$11.64, DELTA = .8625, and THETA = -7.7191. The long bull spread with calls consists of buying the call with the lower exercise price (Call B) and selling the call with the higher exercise price (Call A). The spread costs $11.64 - $1.82 = $9.82. The DELTA of the spread equals $DELTA_B$ - $DELTA_A$ = .8625 - .2735 = .5890. If the stock price is $60 at expiration, Call B will be worth $10, and Call A will expire worthless. If the stock price remains at $60, the value of the spread will have to move from $9.82 now to $10.00 at expiration, so the THETA for the spread must be positive. This can be confirmed by computing the two THETAs and noting: $THETA_A$ = -8.9173 and $THETA_B$ = -7.7191. For the spread, we buy Call B and sell Call A, giving a THETA for the spread of -7.7191 - (-8.9173) = 1.1982.

8. Consider again the sample options, $C2$ and $P2$, of the chapter discussion as given in Table 14.7. Assume now that the stock pays a continuous dividend of 3 percent per annum. See if you can tell how the sensitivities will differ for the call and a put without computing. Now compute the DELTA, GAMMA, VEGA, THETA, and RHO of the two options if the stock has a dividend.

    The presence of a continuous dividend makes d_1 smaller than it otherwise would be, because the continuous dividend rate, δ, is subtracted in the numerator of d_1. With a smaller d_1, $N(d_1)$ is also smaller. But, $N(d_1)$ = DELTA for a call, so the DELTA of a call will be smaller with a dividend present. By the same reasoning, the DELTA of the put must increase.

Sensitivity	C2	P2
DELTA	.5794	-.4060
GAMMA	.0182	.0182
THETA	-10.3343	-5.5997
VEGA	26.93	26.93
RHO	23.9250	-23.4823

9. Consider three calls Call C, Call D, and Call E, all written on the same underlying stock. $S =$ $80; $r = .07$; $\sigma = .2$. For Call C, $X = \$70$, and $T - t = 90$ days. For Call D, $X = \$75$, and $T - t =$ 90 days. For Call E, $X = \$80$, and $T - t = 120$ days. Compute the price, DELTA, and GAMMA for each of these calls. Using Calls C and D, create a DELTA-neutral portfolio assuming that the position is long one Call C. Now use calls C, D, and E to form a portfolio that is DELTA-neutral and GAMMA-neutral, again assuming that the portfolio is long one Call C.

Measure	Call C	Call D	Call E
Price	$11.40	$7.16	$4.60
DELTA	.9416	.8088	.6018
GAMMA	.0147	.0343	.0421

For a DELTA-neutral portfolio comprised of Calls C and D that is long one Call C, we must choose a position of Z shares of Call D to satisfy the following equation:

$$.9416 + .8088\, Z = 0$$

Therefore, $Z = -1.1642$, and the portfolio consists of purchasing one Call C and selling 1.1642 units of Call D.

To form a portfolio of Calls C, D, and E that is long one Call C and that is also DELTA-neutral and GAMMA-neutral, the portfolio must meet both of the following conditions, where Y and Z are the number of Call Cs and Call Ds, respectively.

DELTA-neutrality: $.9416 + .8088\, Y + .6018\, Z = 0$
GAMMA-neutrality: $.0147 + .0343\, Y + .0421\, Z = 0$

Multiplying the second equation by (.8088/.0343) gives:

$$.3466 + .8088\, Y + .9927\, Z = 0$$

Subtracting this equation from the DELTA-neutrality equation gives:

$$.5950 - .3909\ Z = 0$$

Therefore, $Z = 1.5221$. Substituting this value of Z into the DELTA-neutrality equation gives:

$$.8088\ Y + .9416 + .6018\ (1.5221) = 0$$

$Y = -2.2968$. Therefore, the DELTA-neutral and GAMMA-neutral portfolio consists of buying one unit of Call C, selling 2.2968 units of Call D, and buying 1.5221 units of Call E.

15
American Option Pricing

Answers to Questions and Problems

1. Explain why American and European calls on a non-dividend stock always have the same value.

    An American option is just like a European option, except the American option carries the right of early exercise. Exercising a call before expiration discards the time value inherent in the option. The only offsetting benefit from early exercise arises from an attempt to capture a dividend. If there is no dividend, there is no incentive to early exercise, so the early exercise feature of an American call on a non-dividend stock has no value.

2. Explain why American and European puts on a non-dividend stock can have different values.

    The exercise value of a put is $X - S$. On a European put, this value cannot be captured until the expiration date. Therefore, before expiration the value of the European put will be a function of the present value of these exercise proceeds: $e^{-r(T-)t}(X - S)$. The American put gives immediate access at any time to the full proceeds, $X - S$, through exercise. In certain circumstances, notably on puts that are deep-in-the-money with time remaining until expiration, this differential in exercise conditions can give the American put extra value over the corresponding European put, even in the absence of dividends.

3. Explain the circumstances that might make the early exercise of an American put on a non-dividend stock desirable.

    Early exercise of an American put provides the holder with an immediate cash inflow of $X - S$. These proceeds can earn a return from the date of exercise to the expiration date that is not available on a European put. However, early exercise discards the time value of the put. Therefore, the early exercise decision requires trading off the sacrificed time value against the interest that can be earned by investing the exercise value from the date of exercise to the expiration date of the put. For deep-in-the-money puts with time remaining until expiration, the potential interest gained can exceed the time value of the put that is sacrificed.

4. What factors might make an owner exercise an American call?

    The key factor is an approaching dividend, and exercise of an American call should occur only at the moment before an ex-dividend date. The dividend must be "large"relative to the share price, and the call will typically also be deep-in-the-money.

5. Do dividends on the underlying stock make the early exercise of an American put more or less likely? Explain.

    Dividends make early exercise of an American put less likely. Dividends decrease the stock price and increase the exercise value of the put. Thus, the holder of the American put has an incentive to delay exercising and wait for the dividend payments.

6. Do dividends on the underlying stock make the early exercise of an American call more or less likely? Explain.

    Dividends increase the likelihood of early exercise on an American call. In fact, if there are no dividends on the underlying stock, early exercise of an American call is irrational.

7. Explain the strategy behind the pseudo-American call pricing strategy.

    In pseudo-American call pricing, the analysis treats the stock price as the current stock price reduced by the present value of all dividends to occur before the option expires. It then considers potential exercise just prior to each ex-dividend date, by reducing the exercise price by the present value of all dividends to be paid, including the imminent dividend. (The dividends are a reduction from the exercise price because they represent a cash inflow if the option is exercised.) For each dividend date, the analysis values a European option using the Black-Scholes model. The pseudo-American price is the maximum of these European option prices. Implicitly, the pricing strategy assumes exercise on the date that gives the highest European option price.

8. Consider a stock with a price of $140 and a standard deviation of .4. The stock will pay a dividend of $2 in 40 days and a second dividend of $2 in 130 days. The current risk-free rate of interest is 10 percent. An American call on this stock has an exercise price of $150 and expires in 100 days. What is the price of the call according to the pseudo-American approach?

    First, notice that the second dividend is scheduled to be paid in 130 days, after the option expires. Therefore, the second dividend cannot affect the option price and it may be disregarded. To apply the pseudo-American model, we begin by subtracting the present value of the dividend from the stock price to form the adjusted stock price:

    Adjusted stock price = $140 - $2 $e^{-.10(40/365)}$ = $138.02

For the single dividend date, we reduce the exercise price by the $2 of dividend so the adjusted exercise price is $148. Applying the Black-Scholes model with $S = \$138.02$, $E = \$148$, $T - t = 40$ days, gives a price of $4.05. Applying the Black-Scholes model with $S = \$138.02$, $E = \$150$, $T - t = 100$, gives a price of $8.29. The higher price, $8.29, is the pseudo-American option price.

9. Could the exact American call pricing model be used to price the option in Question 8? Explain.

    Yes. Once we notice that the second dividend falls beyond the expiration date of the option, the exact American model fits exactly and gives a price of $8.28, almost the same as the pseudo-American price of $8.29.

10. Explain why the exact American call pricing model treats the call as an "option on an option."

    The exact American model applies to call options on stocks with a single dividend occurring before the option expires. Early exercise of an American call is optimal only at the ex-dividend date. At the ex-dividend date, the holder of an American call has a choice: exercise and own the stock or do not exercise and hold what is then equivalent to a European option that expires at the original expiration date of the American call. (The option that results from not exercising is equivalent to a European call because there are no more dividends occurring before expiration.) Thus, the exact American call model recognizes that the call embodies an option to own a European option at the dividend date. It also embodies the right to acquire the stock at the stated exercise price at the ex-dividend date.

11. Explain the idea of a bivariate cumulative standardized normal distribution. What would be the cumulative probability of observing two variables both with a value of zero, assuming that the correlation between them was zero? Explain.

    The bivariate cumulative distribution considers the probability of two standardized normal variates having values equal to or below a certain threshold at the same time given a certain correlation between the two. Consider first a univariate standardized normal variate. The probability of its value being zero or less equals the chance that it is below its mean of zero, which is 50 percent. Considering two such variates, with a zero correlation between them, the probability that both have a value of zero or less equals $.5 \times .5 = .25$. If the two variables had a correlation other than zero, this probability would be different.

12. In the exact American call pricing model, explain why the model can compute the call price with only one dividend.

    The exact American model uses the cumulative bivariate standardized normal distribution, which considers the correlation between a pair of variates. The formula, for example, evaluates the probability of not exercising and the option finishing in the money, and of not exercising and the option finishing out of the money. If there were more dividends, the bivariate distribution would be inadequate to handle all of the possible combinations and higher multivariate normal distributions would have to be considered. For these, the no solution has yet been found.

13. What is the critical stock price in the exact American call pricing model?

   The critical stock price, S^*, is the stock price that makes the call owner indifferent regarding exercise at the ex-dividend date. If the option is not exercised at the ex-dividend date, the American call effectively becomes a European call and the value is simply given by the Black-Scholes model. If the owner exercises, she receives the stock price, plus the dividend, less the exercise price. Therefore, where D_1 is the dividend, the critical stock price makes the following equation hold:

$$S^* + D_1 - X = \text{European call}$$

14. Explain how the analytical approximation for American option values is analogous to the Merton model.

   Both models pertain to underlying goods with a continuous dividend rate.

15. Explain the role of the critical stock price in the analytic approximation for an American call.

   The critical stock price is the stock price that makes the owner of an American call indifferent regarding exercise. If the stock price exceeds the critical stock price, the owner should exercise. Otherwise, the option should not be exercised.

16. Why should an American call owner exercise if the stock price exceeds the critical price?

   If the stock price exceeds the critical stock price, the owner should exercise to capture the exercise proceeds. These can be invested to earn a return from the date of exercise to the expiration of the option. The critical stock price is the price at which the benefits of earning that interest just equals the costs of discarding the time value of the option. If the stock price exceeds the critical stock price, the potential interest proceeds are worth more than the time value of the option, and the option should be exercised.

17. Consider the binomial model for an American call and put on a stock that pays no dividends. The current stock price is \$120, and the exercise price for both the put and the call is \$110. The standard deviation of the stock returns is .4, and the risk-free rate is 10 percent. The options expire in 120 days. Model the price of these options using a four-period tree. Draw the stock tree and the corresponding trees for the call and the put. Explain when, if ever, each option should be exercised. What is the value of a European call in this situation? Can you find the value of the European call without making a separate computation? Explain.

$U = 1.1215$; $D = .8917$; $\pi_U = .5073$. The American call is worth \$18.93, while the American put is worth \$5.48. With no dividend, the American call should not be exercised at any time. The put should be exercised if the stock price drops three times from \$120.00 to \$85.07. Then the exercisable proceeds would be \$24.93, but the corresponding European put would be worth only \$24.03. The asterisk in the option tree indicates a node at which exercise should occur.

Stock and Call Price Lattices for Problem 17

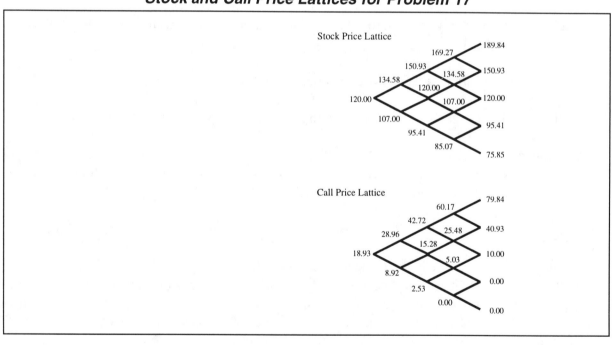

Put Price Lattice for Problem 17

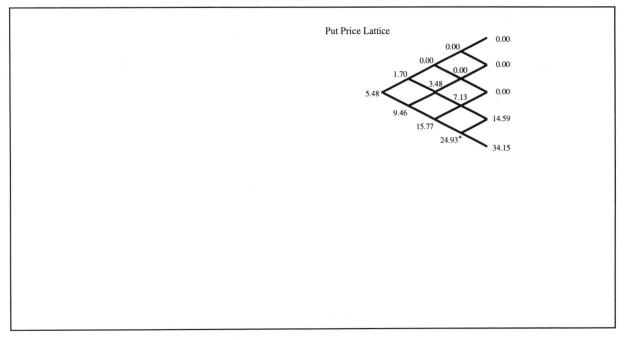

Put Price Lattice

18. Consider the binomial model for an American call and put on a stock whose price is $120. The exercise price for both the put and the call is $110. The standard deviation of the stock returns is .4, and the risk-free rate is 10 percent. The options expire in 120 days. The stock will pay a dividend equal to 3 percent of its value in 50 days. Model and compute the price of these options using a four-period tree. Draw the stock tree and the corresponding trees for the call and the put. Explain when, if ever, each option should be exercised.

$U = 1.1215; D = .8917; \pi_U = .5073$. The call is worth $16.14, and the put is worth $6.28. The call should never be exercised. The put should be exercised if the stock price drops three straight times to $82.52. This gives exercisable proceeds of $27.48, compared to a computed value of $26.58. The asterisk in the option tree indicates a node at which exercise should occur.

Stock and Call Price Lattices for Problem 18

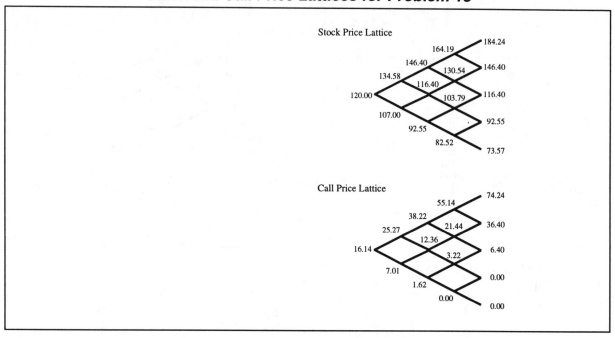

Put Price Lattice for Problem 18

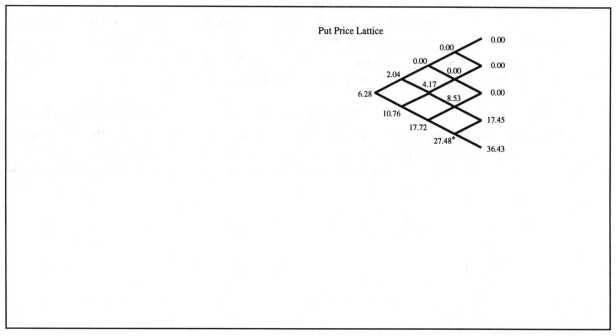

19. Consider the binomial model for an American call and put on a stock whose price is $120. The exercise price for both the put and the call is $110. The standard deviation of the stock returns is .4, and the risk-free rate is 10 percent. The options expire in 120 days. The stock will pay a $3 dividend in 50 days. Model and compute the price of these options using a four-period tree. Draw the stock tree and the corresponding trees for the call and the put. Explain when, if ever, each option should be exercised.

$U = 1.1215$; $D = .8917$; $\pi_U = .5073$. The call is worth $16.63, while the put is worth $6.14. The call should never be exercised. The put should be exercised if the stock price drops three straight times to $82.97. This gives exercisable proceeds of $27.03, which exceeds the computed value of $26.13. The asterisk in the option tree indicates a node at which exercise should occur.

Stock and Adjusted Stock Price Lattices for Problem 19

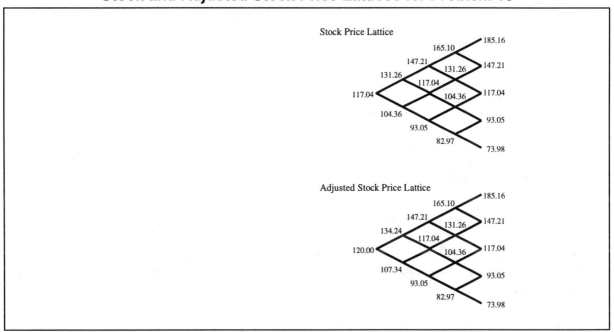

Call and Put Price Lattices for Problem 19

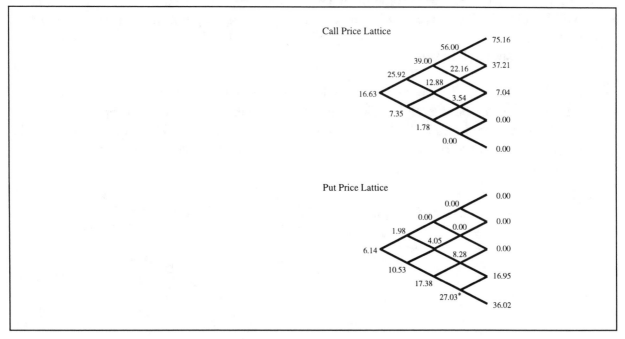

20. Consider the analytic approximation for American options. A stock sells for $130, has a standard deviation of .3, and pays a continuous dividend of 3 percent. An American call and put on this stock both have an exercise price of $130, and they both expire in 180 days. The risk-free rate is 12 percent. Find the value of the call and put according to this model. Demonstrate that you have found the correct critical stock price for both options.

For the call, the critical price is $S* = \$604.08$. For the put, the critical price is $S** = \$103.88$. To verify that these critical prices are correct, we need to show that they satisfy the following two equations.

Call: $\quad S^* - X = c_t(S^*, X, T - t) + \{1 - e^{-\delta(T-t)}N(d_1)\}(S^*/q_2)$

Put: $\quad X - S^{**} = p_t(S^{**}, X, T - t) - [1 - e^{-\delta(T-t)}N(-d_1)](S^{**}/q_1)$

$$q_1 = \frac{1 - n - \sqrt{(n-1)^2 + 4k}}{2}$$

$$q_2 = \frac{1 - n + \sqrt{(n - 1)^2 + 4k}}{2}$$

$$n = \frac{2(r - \delta)}{\sigma^2}, \quad k = \frac{2r}{\sigma^2(1 - e^{-r(T - t)})}$$

With these values:

$$n = 2(.12 - .03)/(.3 \times .3) = 2.00$$

$$k = (2 \times .12)/[.3 \times .3 (1 - .9425)] = .24/.0052 = 46.4082$$

$$q_1 = \frac{1 - 2 - \sqrt{(2 - 1)^2 + 4(46.4082)}}{2} = -7.3307$$

$$q_2 = \frac{1 - 2 + \sqrt{(2 - 1)^2 + 4(46.4082)}}{2} = 6.3307$$

For the call, evaluating d_1 at the critical price for the call, \$604.08, gives $d_1 = 35.4167$:

$$d_1 = \frac{\ln\left(\frac{604.08}{130}\right) + [.12 - .03 + .5(.3)(.3)]\left(\frac{180}{365}\right)}{.3\sqrt{\frac{180}{365}}} = 35.4167$$

For the put, evaluating d_1 at the critical price for the put, \$103.88, gives $d_1 = -.7487$:

$$d_1 = \frac{\ln\left(\frac{103.88}{130}\right) + [.12 - .03 + .5(.3)(.3)]\left(\frac{180}{365}\right)}{.3\sqrt{\frac{180}{365}}} = -.7487$$

For the call, $N(d_1) = N(35.4167) = 1.0000$, while for the put, $N(-d_1) = N(-27.0603) = .772981$. The prices of the corresponding European call and put, each evaluated at its critical price, are $472.68 and $22.74, respectively.

With these values, we now verify that the specified critical prices are correct. For the call:

$$604.08 - 130.00 = 474.08 = 472.68 + (.0147)(604.08/6.3307)$$

For the put:

$$130.00 - 103.88 = 26.12 = 22.74 - (.2384)(103.88/-7.3307)$$

21. An American call and put both have an exercise price of $100. An acquaintance asserts that the critical stock price for both options is $90 under the analytic approximation technique. Comment on this claim and explain your reasoning.

    Something is amiss. The critical price for a call must lie above the exercise price, while the critical price for a put must lie below the exercise price. Therefore, $90 might be the critical price for the put, but it cannot be the critical price for the call.

16
Options on Stock Indexes, Foreign Currency, and Futures

Answers to Questions and Problems

1. Explain why interest payments on a foreign currency can be treated as analogous to a dividend on a common stock.

    For a stock, dividends represent a leakage of value from the asset. If dividends were not paid, the stock price would continue to grow at a higher rate, compounding the value of the dividends. The same is true for a currency. The interest rate paid by a currency represents a leakage of value from the currency. Therefore, dividends from common stock and interest payments from a currency can be treated in the same way for option pricing purposes.

2. Why do we assume that the cost-of-carry for a futures is the same as the risk-free rate?

    For pricing options on futures, the important consideration is that the futures price follow the cost-of-carry relationship very closely. This adherence to the cost-of-carry model is much more important than the exact amount of the cost-of-carry. The option pricing model for futures does not work well if there is not an adherence to the cost-of-carry model. Thus, it is mainly a matter of convenience that we assume the cost-of-carry to equal the risk-free rate. In the real world, this assumption performs very well for financial futures, but it performs less well for futures on agricultural goods.

3. Explain how to adjust a price lattice for an underlying good that makes discrete payments.

    The text considers three types of dividend payments: constant proportional payments, occasional payments equal to a percentage of the asset value, and occasional payments of a fixed dollar amount. In every case, the presence of the dividend requires an adjustment in the stock price lattice. In essence, the nodes in the stock price lattice must be decreased by the present value of the dividends that will occur from the time represented by that node until the expiration of the option. Dividends occurring after the expiration date of the option play no role and may be disregarded. Once the stock price lattice has been adjusted to reflect the dividends, the corresponding lattice for the put or call can be worked through in the normal way to price the option correctly.

4. If a European and an American call on the same underlying good have different prices when all of the terms of the two options are identical, what does this difference reveal about the two options? What does it mean if the two options have identical prices?

    If the two have an identical price, it means that the early exercise feature of the American option has no value. Any difference in the prices will stem from the value associated with the early exercise privilege.

5. Consider an option on a futures contract within the context of the binomial model. Assume that the futures price is 100.00, that the risk-free interest rate is 10 percent, that the standard deviation of the futures is .4, and that the futures expires in one year. Assuming that a call and a put on the futures also expire in one year, compute the binomial parameters U, D, and π_U. Now compute the expected futures price in one period. What does this reveal about the expected movement in futures prices?

$$U = e^{.4\sqrt{1}} = 1.4918 ; \quad D = \frac{1}{U} = .6703$$

$$\pi_U = \frac{e^{(.10 - .10)\,1} - .6703}{1.4918 - .6703} = .4013$$

The expected price movement is:

$$.4013\,(1.4918) + .5987\,(.6703) = 1.00$$

Thus, the futures price is not expected to change over the next year. In general, this will be true for futures. The futures price already impounds the expected price change in the asset between the current date and the expiration of the futures contract.

6. For a call and a put option on a foreign currency, compute the Merton model price, the binomial model price for a European option with three periods, the Barone-Adesi and Whaley model price, and the binomial model price with three periods for American options. Data are as follows: The foreign currency value is 2.5; the exercise price on all options is 2.0; the time until expiration is 90 days; the risk-free rate of interest is 7 percent; the foreign interest rate is 4 percent; the standard deviation of the foreign currency is .2.

The prices in the following table show that the American call and put have no exercise potential. The difference between the Merton and Whaley model put prices, on the one hand, and the binomial model put prices, on the other, are due to the very few periods being employed.

	Merton Model	European Binomial	Whaley Model	American Binomial
Call	.5104	.5097	.5104	.5097
Put	.0008	0	.0008	0

7. Consider a call and a put on a stock index. The index price is 500.00, and the two options expire in 120 days. The standard deviation of the index is .2, and the risk-free rate of interest is 7 percent. The two options have a common exercise price of 500.00. The stock index will pay a dividend of 20.00 index units in 40 days. Find the European and American option prices according to the binomial model, assuming two periods. Be sure to draw the lattices for the stock index and for all of the options that are being priced.

$$U = e^{.2\sqrt{\frac{60}{365}}} = 1.0845 ; \quad D = \frac{1}{1.0845} = .9221$$

$$\pi_U = \frac{1.0116 - .9221}{1.0845 - .9221} = .5510$$

As the following price lattices show, the European and American calls are worth $19.19. The European put is worth $27.67, and the American put is worth $30.21.

Stock Price Lattice for Problem 7

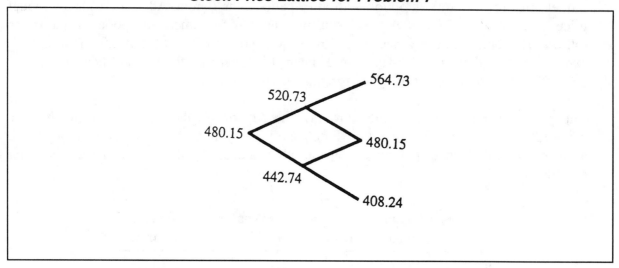

Adjusted Stock Price Lattice for Problem 7

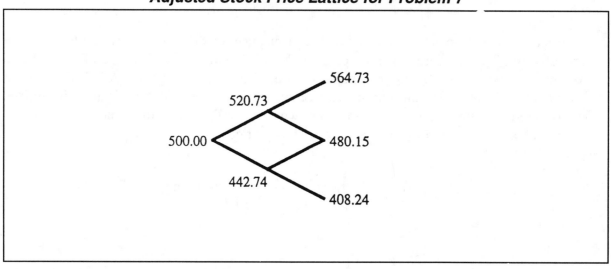

Call Price Lattice for Problem 7

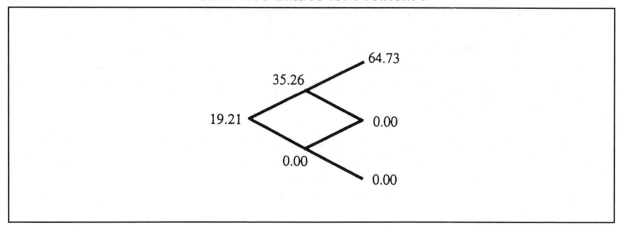

European Put Price Lattice for Problem 7

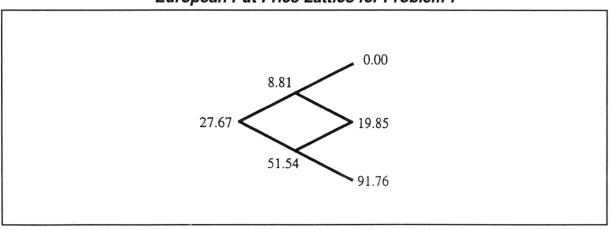

American Put Price Lattice for Problem 7

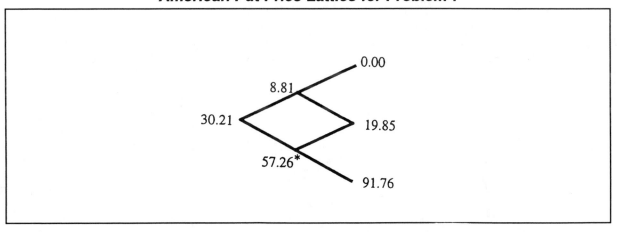

8. Consider two European calls and two European put options on a foreign currency. The exercise prices are $.90 and $1.00, giving a total of four options. All options expire in one year. The current risk-free rate is 8 percent, the foreign interest rate is 5 percent, and the standard deviation of the foreign currency is .3. The foreign currency is priced at $.80. Find all four option prices according to the Merton model. Compare the ratio of the option prices to the ratio of the exercise prices. What does this show?

   With $X = \$.90$, the call is worth $.0640, and the put is worth $.1338. With $X = \$1.00$, the call is worth $.0392, and the put is worth $.2014. Comparing the ratio of the option prices to the ratio of exercise prices shows that the call is more sensitive to a change in the exercise price than is the put. A change of about 10 percent in the exercise price causes about a 63 percent change in the call price, but only about a 51 percent change in the put price.

17

The Options Approach to Corporate Securities

Answers to Questions and Problems

1. Explain why common stock is itself like a call option. In the option analysis of common stock, what plays the role of the exercise price and what plays the role of the underlying stock?

   Common stock is like a call option on the entire firm. To see how this can be the case, consider a firm with a single bond issue outstanding and assume that the bond is a pure discount bond. When the bond matures, the common stockholders have a choice: They can pay the bondholders the promised payment or they can surrender the firm to the bondholders. If the firm is worth more than the amount due to the bondholders, the stock owners will pay the bondholders and keep the excess. If the firm is worth less than the amount due to the bondholders, the stock owners will abandon the firm to the bond owners.

   In this situation, the amount due to the bond owners plays the role of the exercise price. The maturity date of the bond is the expiration date of the call option represented by the common stock. The common stock is like a call option. At expiration, the stock owners can exercise their call option by paying the claim of the bondholders (the exercise price). Upon exercising, the stockholders receive the underlying asset (the entire firm).

2. Consider a firm that issues a pure discount bond that matures in one year and has a face value of $1,000,000. Analyze the payoffs that the bondholders will receive in option pricing terms, assuming the only other security in the firm is common stock.

   When the bond matures, the stock owners decide whether to pay the bonds or surrender the firm to the bond holders in lieu of payment. If the value of the firm exceeds the amount owed to the bond owners, $1,000,000, the bond holders receive full payment and the stock owners retain the excess. If the firm's value is less than the promised payment, the stock owners abandon the firm and the bond holders receive a payment equal to the value of the entire firm. However, by hypothesis, this is less than the promised payment of $1,000,000. This pattern of payment is like the payments on a short put position with an exercise price that equals the face value of the bond. However, a short position in a put can give a payoff at expiration that is negative. This is not true of a bond. The worst payoff for the bond is zero. Therefore, the payoff has the same pattern as a short position in a put with an exercise price that equals the face value of the bond plus a long position in a riskless bond.

3. Consider a firm with common stock and a pure discount bond as its financing. The total value of the firm is $1,000,000. There are 10,000 shares of common stock priced at $70 per share. The bond matures in ten years and has a total face value of $500,000. What is the interest rate on the bond, assuming annual compounding? Would the interest rate become higher or lower if the volatility of the firm's cash flows increases?

    The $1,000,000 value of the firm equals the sum of the stock and bond values. As the outstanding stock is worth $700,000, the bonds must be worth $300,000. Therefore, the interest rate is 5.24 percent. If the volatility of the firm's cash flows increases, the total value of the firm will not change. However, because the common stock can be analyzed as a call option on the firm, the value of the common stock must increase. This means that the value of the bonds must decrease. If the bond value decreases, its yield must increase. This makes sense, because the bonds should be worth less if the firm's cash flows become more risky.

4. A firm has a capital structure consisting of common stock and a single bond. The managers of the firm are considering a major capital investment that will be financed from internally generated funds. The project can be initiated in two ways, one with a high fixed cost component and the other with a low fixed cost component. Although both technologies have the same expected value, the high fixed cost approach has the potential for greater payoffs. (If the product is successful, the high fixed cost approach gives much lower total costs for large production levels.) What does option theory suggest about the choice the managers should make? Explain.

    Assuming that the managers perform in the interest of their shareholders, they must make the decision that increases the value of the stock. As the stock represents a call option on the total firm value, the managers should prefer the higher operating leverage/higher operating risk strategy.

5. In a firm with common stock, senior debt, and subordinated debt, assume that both debt instruments mature at the same time. What is the necessary condition on the value of the firm at maturity for each security holder to receive at least some payment? With two classes of debt, does option theory counsel managers to increase the riskiness of the firm's operations? Would there be any difference on this point between a firm with a single debt issue and two debt issues? Which bondholders would tend to be more risk averse as far as choosing a risk level for the firm's operations? Explain.

    For the senior debtholders to receive some payment, the value of the firm must exceed zero. For the subordinated debtholders to receive some payment, the value of the firm must exceed the total owed to the senior debtholders. For the common stock holders to receive any payment, the value of the firm must exceed the amount owed on both classes of debt. If the managers perform in the interest of the stockholders, the mere presence of two classes of debt does not suggest a change in operating policy. The stockholders get paid only after all the bondholders are paid, so it does not matter to the stockholders how the debt is split up, but only how much the total amount of debt payments is. Given that the junior debtholders have already purchased the junior debt, they are (by revealed preference) more risk tolerant than the holders of the senior debt. However, increasing operating risk transfers wealth away from bondholders to stockholders. Thus, the junior debtholders would probably prefer a low risk operating strategy if funds would be certain to sufficiently cover their holdings. However, consider an operating policy that would only generate enough cash to pay the senior debtholders. In this situation, it is clear that the junior debtholders would prefer a more risky operating policy that might give sufficient payoffs to repay their obligations.

6. Consider a firm financed solely by common stock and a single callable bond issue. Assume that the bond is a pure discount bond. Is there any circumstance in which the firm should call the bond before the maturity date? Would such an exercise of the firm's call option discard the time premium? Explain.

    The stockholders should wait until the maturity date. The stockholders' situation here is analogous to a call on a non-dividend stock. Early payment of the bond discards the time premium inherent in the option they hold.

7. Consider a firm financed only by common stock and a convertible bond issue. When should the bondholders exercise? Explain. If the common shares pay a dividend, could it make sense for the bondholders to exercise before the bond matures? Explain by relating your answer to our discussion of the exercise of American calls on dividend-paying stocks.

    If the common stock pays no dividend, the bondholders should not exercise until the last possible date. However, if the stock pays a sufficiently large dividend, it might pay the bondholders to convert earlier. The bondholder holds a call option on the firm's shares. If those shares pay dividends, then they are leaking value. The bondholders must decide whether it is worthwhile to discard the time premium in favor of securing the dividend. This is exactly analogous to the problem faced by the holder of an American call option on a dividend paying stock.

8. Warrants are often used to compensate top executives in firms. Often these warrants cannot be exercised until a distant expiration date. This form of compensation is used to align the manager's incentives with the maximization of the shareholders' wealth. Explain how the manager's receiving warrants might thwart the efforts to change his or her incentives.

If a manager holds warrants, and the value of these warrants is large relative to other forms of compensation, the manager will focus on maximizing the value of the firm at the expiration date of the warrants. This incentive might be incompatible with making decisions that will increase the value of the firm at other dates. For example, if markets are not perfect, then the value of the shares might not fully reflect a good decision to make a large capital budgeting outlay. Therefore, the manager might forego the investment in order to enhance the share price on the critical date for the manager.

18
Exotic Options

Answers to Questions and Problems

1. Using the following parameter values, find the price of a Forward-Start Put: $S = 100$; $X = 100$; $T - t = 1$ year; $\sigma = 0.2$; $r = 0.1$; $\delta = 0.05$ tg $= 0.5$.

The first step is to value a plain vanilla put on the grant date, which is in one half year. At that time, the put will have a half year remaining until expiration. Therefore,

$$d_1^M = \frac{\ln\left(\dfrac{100}{100}\right) + \left[0.1 - 0.05 + 0.5(0.2)(0.2)\right] (0.5)}{0.2 \sqrt{0.5}} = 0.247487$$

$$d_2^M = 0.247487 - 0.141421 = 0.106066$$

$$
\begin{aligned}
p_{tg}^M &= X\, e^{-r\,(T - t)} N(-d_2^M) - e^{-\delta\,(T - t)} S_t N(-d_1^M) \\
&= 100 e^{-.1\,(0.5)} N(-0.106066) - e^{-0.05\,(0.5)} 100\, N(-0.247487) \\
&= 100 e^{-.1\,(0.5)}\, 0.457765 - e^{-0.05\,(0.5)}\, 100\, (0.402266) \\
&= 4.3106
\end{aligned}
$$

Forward-Start Put $= e^{-\delta(tg - t)} P_{tg}^M = e^{-.05(.5)}\, 4.3106 = 4.2042$

2. Price all four types of compound options assuming the following parameter values: S = 100; σ = 0.4; r = 0.1; δ = 0.05; X = 100; x = 8; T = 1 year te = 0.25 years.

The first, and most difficult step, is to find the critical prices for the underlying calls and puts. For underlying calls, we have:

$$S^* e^{-\delta(T - te)} N(z) - X e^{-r(T - te)} N\!\left(z - \sigma\sqrt{T - te}\right) - x = 0$$

For underlying puts, the critical stock price satisfies the following relationship:

$$-S^* e^{-\delta(T - te)} N(-z) + X e^{-r(T - te)} N(-z + \sigma\sqrt{T - te}) - x = 0$$

where:

$$z = \frac{\ln\!\left(\dfrac{S^*}{X}\right) + (r - \delta + 0.5\sigma^2)\,(T - te)}{\sigma\sqrt{T - te}}$$

These critical stock prices must be found by an iterative search. The critical stock price for an underlying call is 86.6162, and for an underlying put the critical stock price is 110.1995. These values can be verified as follows, first for underlying calls:

$$z = \frac{\ln\!\left(\dfrac{86.6152}{100}\right) + (0.1 - 0.05 + 0.5(0.4)\,(0.4))\,(0.75)}{0.4\sqrt{0.75}} = -0.133353$$

Therefore,

$$N(z) = -0.133353; \quad N(z - \sigma\sqrt{T - te}) = -0.479763$$

Thus, we verify that 86.6152 is the correct critical stock price for underlying calls:

$$86.6152\ e^{-0.05\,(0.75)}\,0.446957 - 100\,e^{-0.1\,(0.75)}\,0.315698 - 8 = 0$$

The same verification can be performed for underlying puts.
    Before computing the actual option values, we must compute other intermediate results:

$$w_1 = \frac{\ln\left(\dfrac{S}{S^*}\right) + (r - \delta + 0.5\sigma^2)\,(te - t)}{\sigma\,\sqrt{te - t}}$$

$$w_2 = \frac{\ln\left(\dfrac{S}{X}\right) + (r - \delta + 0.5\sigma^2)\,(T - t)}{\sigma\sqrt{T - t}}$$

With our sample values, $w_1 = 0.880974$ for underlying calls and $w_1 = -0.323111$ for underlying puts. The other intermediate variables are invariant across all option types: $w_2 = 0.325000$; $\rho = 0.5$. We also need the following bivariate cumulative normal probabilities for compound options on underlying calls:

$$N_2(w_1\,;\,w_2\,;\,\rho) = N_2(0.880974;\ 0.325;\ 0.5)$$

$$= 0.564506$$

$$N_2(w_1 - \sigma\sqrt{te - t}\,;\,w_2 - \sigma\sqrt{T - t}\,;\,\rho) = N_2(0.680974;\ -0.075;\ 0.5)$$

$$= 0.416949$$

$$N_2(-w_1\,;\,w_2\,;\,-\rho) = N_2(-0.880974;\ 0.325;\ -0.5)$$

$$= 0.062904$$

$$N_2(-w_1 + \sigma\sqrt{te - t}\,;\,w_2 - \sigma\sqrt{T - t}\,;\,-\rho) = N_2(-0.680974;\ -0.075;\ -0.5)$$

$$= 0.053158$$

$$N(w_1 - \sigma\sqrt{te - t}\,) = N(0.680974\,) = 0.752056$$

$$N(-w_1 + \sigma\sqrt{te - t}\,) = N(-0.680974\,) = 0.247944$$

For convenience, we also note:

$$S e^{-\delta(T-t)} = 100 e^{-0.05(1)} = 95.122942$$

$$X e^{-r(T-t)} = 100 e^{-0.1(1)} = 90.483742$$

$$x e^{-r(te-t)} = 8 e^{-0.1(0.25)} = 7.802479$$

With all of these preliminary calculations out of the way, we are ready to compute the price of compound options on underlying calls from our pricing formulas:

$$CC_t = S e^{-\delta(T-t)} N_2(w_1; w_2; \rho) -$$

$$X e^{-r(T-t)} N_2(w_1 - \sigma\sqrt{te-t}; w_2 - \sigma\sqrt{T-t}; \rho) -$$

$$x e^{-r(te-t)} N(w_1 - \sigma\sqrt{te-t})$$

$$PC_t = -S e^{-\delta(T-t)} N_2(-w_1; w_2; -\rho) +$$

$$X e^{-r(T-t)} N_2(-w_1 + \sigma\sqrt{te-t}; w_2 - \sigma\sqrt{T-t}; -\rho) +$$

$$x e^{-r(te-t)} N(-w_1 + \sigma\sqrt{te-t})$$

$$CC_t = 95.122942(0.564506) - 90.483742(0.416949) - 7.802479(0.752056)$$

$$= 10.1024$$

$$PC_t = -95.122942(0.062904) + 90.483742(0.053158) + 7.802479(0.247944)$$

$$= 0.7608$$

We now turn to the pricing of compound options on underlying puts. Earlier we noted that the critical price is 110.1995 and the appropriate value for w_1 is -0.323111. The probabilities that we need for the underlying puts are:

$$N_2(-w_1; \; -w_2; \; \rho) \; = \; N_2(0.323111; \; -0.325; \; 0.5)$$

$$= \; 0.305486$$

$$N_2(-w_1 + \sigma\sqrt{te-t}; \; -w_2 + \sigma\sqrt{T-t}; \; \rho) \; = \; N_2(0.523111; \; 0.075; \; 0.5)$$

$$= \; 0.442964$$

$$N_2(w_1; \; -w_2; \; -\rho) \; = \; N_2(-0.323111; \; -0.325; \; -0.5)$$

$$= \; 0.067104$$

$$N_2(w_1 - \sigma\sqrt{te-t}; \; -w_2 + \sigma\sqrt{T-t}; \; -\rho) \; = \; N_2(-0.523111; \; 0.075; \; -0.5)$$

$$= \; 0.086930$$

$$N(-w_1 + \sigma\sqrt{te-t}) \; = \; N(0.523111)$$

$$= \; 0.699552$$

$$N(w_1 - \sigma\sqrt{te-t}) \; = \; N(-0.523111)$$

$$= \; 0.300448$$

We can now apply our formulas to compute the values of the compound options on underlying puts.

$$CP_t \; = \; -S \; e^{-\delta(T-t)} \, N_2(-w_1; \; -w_2; \; \rho) \; +$$

$$Xe^{-r(T-t)} \, N_2(-w_1 + \sigma\sqrt{te-t}; \; -w_2 + \sigma\sqrt{T-t}; \; \rho) \; -$$

$$x \, e^{-r(te-t)} \, N(-w_1 + \sigma\sqrt{te-t})$$

$$PP_t \; = \; S \; e^{-\delta(T-t)} \, N_2(w_1; \; -w_2; \; -\rho) \; -$$

$$Xe^{-r(T-t)} \, N_2(w_1 - \sigma\sqrt{te-t}; \; -w_2 + \sigma\sqrt{T-t}; \; -\rho) \; +$$

$$x \, e^{-r(te-t)} \, N(w_1 - \sigma\sqrt{te-t})$$

$$CP_t = -95.122942(0.305486) + 90.483742(0.442964) - 7.802479(0.699552) = 5.5641$$

$$PP_t = 95.122942(0.067104) - 90.483742(0.086930) + 7.802479(0.300448) = 0.8617$$

3. Price a simple chooser option based on the following parameter values: S = 100; X = 100; T = 1 year; σ = 0.5; r = 0.1; δ = 0.05; tc = 0.5 years. By comparing this result with that of the example chooser in the sample text, what can you conclude about the influence of the stock's risk on the value of the chooser?

To price the chooser, we must first compute the following parameters:

$$w_1 = \frac{\ln\left(\frac{S}{X}\right) + (r - \delta + 0.5\,\sigma^2)\,(T - t)}{\sigma\sqrt{T - t}}$$

$$= \frac{\ln\left(\frac{100}{100}\right) + (0.1 - 0.05 + 0.5\,(0.5)\,(0.5))\,(1.0)}{0.5\sqrt{1.0}}$$

$$= 0.35$$

$$w_2 = \frac{\ln\left(\frac{S}{X}\right) + (r - \delta)\,(T - t) + 0.5\,\sigma^2\,(tc - t)}{\sigma\sqrt{tc - t}}$$

$$= \frac{\ln\left(\frac{100}{100}\right) + (0.1 - 0.05)\,(1.0) + 0.5\,(0.5)\,(0.5)\,(0.5)}{0.5\sqrt{0.5}}$$

$$= 0.318198$$

$$N(w_1) = N(0.35) = 0.636831$$

$$N(-w_2) = N(-0.318198) = 0.375167$$

$$N(w_1 - \sigma\sqrt{T - t}) = N(0.35 - 0.5) = 0.440382$$

$$N(-w_2 + \sigma\sqrt{tc - t}) = N(-0.318198 + 0.353553) = 0.514102$$

Noting for convenience:

$$Se^{-\delta(T-t)} = 100\,e^{-0.05\,(1.0)} = 95.122942$$
$$Xe^{-r(T-t)} = 100\,e^{-0.1\,(1.0)} = 90.483742$$

We now compute the value of the chooser according to our valuation formula:

$$Chooser_t = Se^{-\delta(T-t)}N(w_1) - Xe^{-r(T-t)}\,N(w_1 - \sigma\sqrt{T-t}\,) +$$
$$Xe^{-r(T-t)}\,N(-w_2 + \sigma\sqrt{tc-t}\,) - S\,e^{-\delta(T-t)}N(-w_2)$$

$$Chooser_t = (95.122942)\,(0.636831) - 90.483742\,(0.440382)$$

$$+\ 90.483742\,(0.514102) - 95.122942\,(0.375167)$$

$$=\ 31.5606$$

The higher the volatility, the greater the value of the chooser option.

4. Find the value of a down-and-in put with: $S = 100$; $X = 100$; $T - t = 1$ year; $\sigma = 0.3$; $r = 0.1$; $\delta = 0.05$; BARR $= 97$; and REBATE $= 2$.

We begin by computing a host of intermediate values:

$$\lambda = \frac{r - \delta + 0.5\,\sigma^2}{\sigma^2} = 1.055556$$

$$w_2 = \frac{\ln\left(\dfrac{S}{BARR}\right)}{\sigma\sqrt{T-t}} + \lambda\,\sigma\sqrt{T-t} = 0.418197$$

$$w_3 = \frac{\ln\left(\dfrac{BARR^2}{SX}\right)}{\sigma\sqrt{T-t}} + \lambda\,\sigma\sqrt{T-t} = 0.113605$$

$$w_4 = \frac{\ln\left(\dfrac{BARR}{S}\right)}{\sigma\sqrt{T-t}} + \lambda\,\sigma\sqrt{T-t} = 0.215136$$

$$N(-w_2 + \sigma\sqrt{T-t}) = N(-0.118197) = 0.452956$$

$$N(-w_2) = N(-0.418197) = 0.337901$$

$$N(w_4 - \sigma\sqrt{T-t}) = N(-0.084864) = 0.466185$$

$$N(w_4) = N(0.215136) = 0.585169$$

$$N(w_3 - \sigma\sqrt{T-t}) = N(-0.186395) = 0.426067$$

$$N(w_3) = N(0.113605) = 0.545225$$

$$N(w_2 - \sigma\sqrt{T-t}) = N(0.118197) = 0.547044$$

$$X\,e^{-r(T-t)} = 90.483742$$

$$S\,e^{-\delta(T-t)} = 95.122942$$

$$\left(\frac{BARR}{S}\right)^{2\lambda} = 0.937721$$

$$\left(\frac{BARR}{S}\right)^{2\lambda-2} = 0.996621$$

$$REBATE\ e^{-r(T-t)} = 1.809675$$

Using the equations from Table 18.2:

$DP2$ = 90.483742 (0.452956) − 95.122942 (0.337901) = 8.843017

$DP3$ = 90.483742 (0.996621) (0.452956) − 95.122942 (0.937721) (0.337901)

= 10.156731

$DP4$ = 90.483742 (0.996621) (0.426067) − 95.122942 (0.937721) (0.545225)

= −10.211536

$DP5$ = 1.809675 [0.547044 − 0.996621 (0.466185)] = 0.149179

Finally, If X > BARR, then from Table 18.5:

$$DIP = DP2 + DP3 - DP4 + DP5$$

$$= 8.843017 - 10.156731 + 10.211536 + 0.149179$$

$$= 9.0468$$

5. Consider a cash-or-nothing call and put, with common parameter values: S = 100; X = 110; T - t = 0.5 years; σ = 0.4; r = 0.1; δ = 0.0; and Z = 200. What is the value of each option? What is the value of a long position in both options? Which items of information given above are not needed to value the portfolio of the two options?

As the first step, we need to determine:

$$d_2^M = \frac{\ln\left(\dfrac{S_t}{X}\right) + \left(r - \delta + .5\,\sigma^2\right)(T - t)}{\sigma\sqrt{T - t}} - \sigma\sqrt{T - t}$$

$$= \frac{\ln\left(\dfrac{100}{110}\right) + \left[0.1 - 0.0 + 0.5\,(0.4)\,(0.4)\right](0.5)}{0.4\sqrt{(0.5)}} - 0.4\sqrt{0.5}$$

$$= -0.301617$$

$N(d_2^M) = N(-0.301617) = 0.3481472$ and $N(-d_2^M) = N(0.301617) = 0.618528$. Therefore,

$$CONC_t = Z\,e^{-r(T-t)}\,N(d_2^M) = 200\,e^{-0.1(0.5)}\,(0.381472) = 72.5735$$

$$CONP_t = Z\,e^{-r(T-t)}\,N(-d_2^M) = 200\,e^{-0.1\,(0.5)}\,(0.618528) = 117.6724$$

The value of d_2^M and the associated probabilities are not necessary to value a portfolio of a cash-or-nothing call and put. The portfolio will pay the cash amount Z at expiration, so the portfolio must be worth the present value of Z at all times:

$$CONC_t + CONP_t = Z\,e^{-r(T-t)} = 72.5735 + 117.6724 = 190.2459$$

6. Consider an asset-or-nothing call and put, with common parameter values: S = 100; X = 110; T - t = 0.5 years; σ = 0.4; r = 0.1; and δ = 0.0. What is the value of each option? What is the value of a long position in both options? Which items of information given above are not needed to value the portfolio of the two options?

First, we compute the value of d_1^M and its associated probabilities:

$$d_1 = \frac{\ln\left(\dfrac{S_t}{X}\right) + \left(r - \delta + .5\,\sigma^2\right)(T - t)}{\sigma\sqrt{T - t}}$$

$$= \frac{\ln\left(\dfrac{100}{110}\right) + \left(0.1 - 0.0 + .5\,(0.4)(0.4)\right)(0.5)}{0.4\sqrt{0.5}}$$

$$= -0.018774$$

$N(d_1^M) = 0.492511$ and $N(-d_1^M) = 0.507490$. Thus,

$$AONC_t = e^{-\delta(T - t)}\,S_t\,N(d_1^M) = e^{-0.0(0.5)}\,100\,(0.492511) = 49.2510$$

$$AONP_t = e^{-\delta(T - t)}\,S_t\,N(-d_1^M) = e^{-0.0(0.5)}\,100\,(0.507484) = 50.7490$$

The value of a portfolio of a call and put will pay the asset at expiration, thus the value of the portfolio is:

$$AONC_t + AONP_t = e^{-\delta(T - t)}\,S_t = e^{-0.0(0.5)}\,100 = 100$$

Therefore, valuing the portfolio does not require knowledge of d_1^M and its associated probabilities.

7. Value a gap call with: S = 100; X = 100; T - t = 0.5 years; σ = 0.5; r = 0.1; δ = 0.03; and g = 7.

The value of a gap call is:

$$GAPC_t = e^{-\delta(T - t)}\,S_t\,N(d_1^M) - (X + g)\,e^{-r(T - t)}\,N(d_2^M)$$

Therefore, we first compute d_1^M, d_2^M, and their associated probabilities:

$$d_1^M = \frac{\ln\left(\frac{100}{100}\right) + \left[0.1 - 0.03 + 0.5\,(0.5)\,(0.5)\right]\,(0.5)}{0.5\,\sqrt{0.5}} = 0.275772$$

$$d_2^M = d_1^M - \sigma\sqrt{T-t} = 0.275772 - 0.5\sqrt{0.5} = -0.077782$$

$N(d_1^M) = N(0.275772) = 0.608638$, and $N(d_2^M) = N(-0.077782) = 0.469001$. Therefore,

$$GAPC_t = e^{-0.03\,(0.5)}\,100\,(0.608638) - (100 + 7)\,e^{-0.1\,(0.5)}\,(0.469001)$$

$$= 12.2221$$

8. Value a supershare with: $S = 100$; $X_L = 95$; $X_H = 110$; $T - t = 0.5$ years; $\sigma = 0.2$; $r = 0.1$; $\delta = 0.05$. By comparing this calculation with the sample supershare of the text, what can you conclude about the value of supershares and the value $X_H - X_L$?

The valuation formula, shown below, requires computing w_L and w_H.

$$SS = \frac{S\,e^{-\delta\,(T-t)}}{X_L}\left[N(w_L) - N(w_H)\right]$$

$$w_L = \frac{\ln\left(\frac{S}{X_L}\right) + (r - \delta + 0.5\sigma^2)\,(T - t)}{\sigma\sqrt{T-t}}$$

$$= \frac{\ln\left(\frac{100}{95}\right) + \left[0.1 - 0.05 + 0.5\,(0.2)\,(0.2)\right]\,0.5}{0.2\,\sqrt{0.5}}$$

$$= 0.610186$$

and:

$$w_H = \frac{\ln\left(\dfrac{S}{X_H}\right) + (r - \delta + 0.5\sigma^2)(T - t)}{\sigma\sqrt{T - t}}$$

$$w_H = \frac{\ln\left(\dfrac{100}{110}\right) + [0.1 - 0.05 + 0.5(0.2)(0.2)](0.5)}{0.2\sqrt{0.5}}$$

$$= -0.426457$$

N(0.610186) = 0.729131, and N(-0.426457) = 0.334887.

$$SS = \frac{100\,e^{-0.05(0.5)}}{95}\left[0.729131 - 0.334887\right] = 0.4047$$

For the text example and this problem, all parameters are the same except for the payoff range. In the text example, the payoff range ran from 100 to 105 with a supershare value of 0.1332, while in this problem it runs from 95 to 105, with a supershare value of 0.4047. Thus, the larger the payoff range, the greater the value of the supershare. This only makes sense, because the broader the payoff range, the greater the chance that the supershare will finish in the money. Notice that it is not only the size of the range but its location. For instance, if the range ran from 0 to 25 the bounds are wider, but this supershare would be worth zero.

9. Find the value of a lookback call and put with the common parameters: $S = 110$; $T - t = 1$ year; $\sigma = 0.25$; $r = 0.08$; and $\delta = 0.0$. For the call, MINPRI = 80. For the put, MAXPRI = 130.

Computing the value of a lookback call requires the following intermediate values:

$$b = \ln\left(\frac{S}{MINPRI}\right) = \ln\left(\frac{110}{80}\right) = 0.318454$$

$$\mu = r - \delta - 0.5\sigma^2 = 0.08 - 0.0 - 0.5\,(0.25)\,(0.25) = 0.048750$$

$$\lambda = \frac{0.5\,\sigma^2}{r - \delta} = \frac{0.5\,(0.25)\,(0.25)}{0.08 - 0.0} = 0.390625$$

$$S\,e^{-\delta(T - t)} = 110\,e^{-0.0(1)} = 110$$

$$MINPRI\,e^{-r(T - t)} = 80\,e^{-0.08\,(1.0)} = 73.849308$$

$$N\left(\frac{b + \mu\,(T - t)}{\sigma\sqrt{T - t}}\right) = N\left(\frac{0.318454 + 0.048750\,(1.0)}{0.25\sqrt{1.0}}\right) = 0.929058$$

$$N\left(\frac{-b + \mu\,(T - t)}{\sigma\sqrt{T - t}}\right) = N\left(\frac{-0.318454 + 0.048750\,(1.0)}{0.25\sqrt{1.0}}\right) = 0.140335$$

$$N\left(\frac{-b - \mu\,(T - t) - \sigma^2\,(T - t)}{\sigma\sqrt{T - t}}\right) =$$

$$N\left(\frac{-0.318454 - 0.048750\,(1.0) - (0.25)\,(0.25)\,(1.0)}{0.25\sqrt{1.0}}\right) = 0.042824$$

The valuation formula for a lookback call is:

$$LBC = S\,e^{-\delta(T - t)} - MINPRI\,e^{-r(T - t)}\,N\left(\frac{b + \mu\,(T - t)}{\sigma\sqrt{T - t}}\right)$$

$$+ MINPRI\,e^{-r(T - t)}\,\lambda\,e^{b(1 - 1/\lambda)}\,N\left(\frac{-b + \mu\,(T - t)}{\sigma\sqrt{T - t}}\right)$$

$$- S\,e^{-\delta(T - t)}\,(1 + \lambda)\,N\left(\frac{-b - \mu\,(T - t) - \sigma^2\,(T - t)}{\sigma\sqrt{T - t}}\right)$$

Applying this to our values gives:

$$LBC = 110 - 73.849308\,(929058)$$

$$+ 73.849308\,(0.237688)\,(0.140335) - 110\,(1.390625)\,(0.042824)$$

$$= 37.3023$$

To value the lookback put, we use many of the same intermediate values. However, for the lookback put the b term is different:

$$b = \ln\left(\frac{S}{MAXPRI}\right) = \ln\left(\frac{110}{130}\right) = -0.167054$$

The cumulative normal values are:

$$N\left(\frac{-b - \mu\,(T - t)}{\sigma\sqrt{T - t}}\right) =$$

$$N\left(\frac{0.167054 - 0.048750\,(1.0)}{0.25\sqrt{1.0}}\right) = 0.681971$$

$$N\left(\frac{b - \mu\,(T - t)}{\sigma\sqrt{T - t}}\right) =$$

$$N\left(\frac{-0.167054 - 0.048750\,(1.0)}{0.25\sqrt{1.0}}\right) = 0.194009$$

$$N\left(\frac{b + \mu\,(T - t) + \sigma^2\,(T - t)}{\sigma\sqrt{T - t}}\right) =$$

$$N\left(\frac{-0.167054 + 0.048750\,(1.0) + (0.25)\,(0.25)\,(1.0)}{0.25\sqrt{1.0}}\right) = -0.223216$$

We also note that:

$$MAXPRI\,e^{-r\,(T - t)} = 120.005125$$

The valuation formula for the lookback put is:

$$LBP = -S e^{-\delta(T-t)} + MAXPRI\, e^{-r(T-t)}\, N\!\left(\frac{-b - \mu(T-t)}{\sigma\sqrt{T-t}}\right)$$

$$- MAXPRI\, e^{-r(T-t)}\, \lambda\, e^{b(1-1/\lambda)}\, N\!\left(\frac{b - \mu(T-t)}{\sigma\sqrt{T-t}}\right)$$

$$+ S e^{-\delta(T-t)}(1+\lambda)\, N\!\left(\frac{b + \mu(T-t) + \sigma^2(T-t)}{\sigma\sqrt{T-t}}\right)$$

With our values we have:

$$LBP = -110 + 120.005125(0.681971)$$

$$- 120.005125\,(0.506920)\,(0.194009) + 110\,(1.390625)\,(0.411683)$$

$$= -110 + 81.840015 - 11.802140 + 62.974634$$

$$= 23.0125$$

10. Find the value of an average price option with these common parameters: S = 100; X = 90; σ = 0.2; r = 0.1; δ = 0.05; t_0 = 0.0; t_1 = 0.5; t_2 = 0.5; and A = 95. Compute the value of the option with observations every two days, h = 2/365. Now compute the value of the option assuming continuous observation, that is, h = 0. Compare these results with the sample option of the chapter. What does this suggest about the value of the option and the frequency of observation?

$$W = A^{\left(\frac{t_1}{t_1 + t_2 + h}\right)}\, S^{\left(\frac{t_2 + h}{t_1 + t_2 + h}\right)}$$

$$= 95^{\left(\frac{0.5}{0.5 + 0.5 + 0.005479}\right)}\, 100^{\left(\frac{0.5 + 0.005479}{0.5 + 0.5 + 0.005479}\right)}$$

$$= 97.481565$$

$$M = \left(t_0 + t_2 \frac{t_2 + h}{2(t_1 + t_2 + h)} \right) [r - \delta - 0.5\sigma^2]$$

$$= \left(0.0 + 0.5 \frac{0.5 + 0.005479}{2(0.5 + 0.5 + 0.005479)} \right) [0.1 - 0.05 - 0.5(0.2)(0.2)]$$

$$= 0.003770$$

$$\Sigma^2 = t_0 + \left(\frac{t_2(t_2 + h)(2t_2 + h)}{6(t_1 + t_2 + h)^2} \right) \sigma^2$$

$$= 0.0 + \left(\frac{0.5(0.5 + 0.005497)[2(0.5) + 0.005497]}{6(0.5 + 0.5 + 0.005497)^2} \right) (0.2)(0.2)$$

$$= 0.001676$$

$$w_1 = \frac{\ln\left(\frac{W}{X} \right) + M}{\Sigma} + \Sigma$$

$$= \frac{\ln\left(\frac{97.481565}{90} \right) + 0.003770}{0.040936} + 0.040936$$

$$= 2.083730$$

We note that $N(w_1) = 0.981408$, and $N(w_1 - \Sigma) = 0.979464$. The valuation formula for an average price option is:

$$AVGPRI = We^{-r(T - t)} e^{(M + 0.5\Sigma^2)} N(w_1) - Xe^{-r(T - t)} N(w_1 - \Sigma)$$

The price of our example option is:

$$AVGPRI = (97.481565)\, e^{-0.1\,(0.5)}\, e^{[0.003770\,+\,0.5\,(0.001676)]}\, (0.981408)$$

$$-90\, e^{-0.1\,(0.5)}\, (0.979464)$$

$$= 91.423703 - 83.852548$$

$$= 7.5711$$

We now compute the price of the same option with h = 0.

$$W = A^{\left(\frac{t_1}{t_1 + t_2 + h}\right)} S^{\left(\frac{t_2 + h}{t_1 + t_2 + h}\right)}$$

$$= 95^{\left(\frac{0.5}{0.5 + 0.5}\right)} 100^{\left(\frac{0.5}{0.5 + 0.5}\right)}$$

$$= 97.46794$$

$$M = \left(t_0 + t_2 \frac{t_2 + h}{2(t_1 + t_2 + h)}\right) [r - \delta - 0.5\sigma^2]$$

$$= \left(0.0 + 0.5 \frac{0.5}{2(0.5 + 0.5)}\right) [0.1 - 0.05 - 0.5\,(0.2)\,(0.2)]$$

$$= 0.003750$$

$$\Sigma^2 = t_0 + \left(\frac{t_2\,(t_2 + h)\,(2\,t_2 + h)}{6\,(t_1 + t_2 + h)^2}\right) \sigma^2$$

$$= 0.0 + \left(\frac{0.5\,(0.5)\,[2\,(0.5)]}{6\,(0.5 + 0.5)^2}\right) (0.2)\,(0.2)$$

$$= 0.001667$$

$$w_1 = \frac{\ln\left(\dfrac{W}{X}\right) + M}{\Sigma} + \Sigma$$

$$= \frac{\ln\left(\dfrac{97.46794}{90}\right) + 0.003750}{0.040829} + 0.040829$$

$$= 2.085264$$

$N(w_1) = 0.981477$, and $N(w_1 - \Sigma) = 0.979545$. The price of our example option with continuous observation is:

$$AVGPRI = (97.46794)\, e^{-0.1\,(0.5)}\, e^{[0.003750\,+\,0.5\,(0.001667)]}\, (0.981477)$$

$$-90\, e^{-0.1\,(0.5)}\, (0.979545)$$

$$= 91.415066 - 83.859482$$

$$= 7.5556$$

For the example average price option of the text and these problems, we find that the value of the option is: 7.5556 with continuous observation; 7.5634 with observations every day; and 7.5711 with observations every second day. This suggests that the price of the average option varies inversely with the observation frequency, but that the effect is quite small.

11. Consider an exchange option with the following common parameter values: $S_1 = 100$; $S_2 = 100$; $\sigma_1 = 0.3$; $\sigma_2 = 0.2$; $\delta_1 = 0.05$; $\delta_2 = 0.05$; $T - t = 0.5$ years. Compute the value of this exchange option with $\rho = 0.0$ and $\rho = 0.7$. Compare your results with those for the sample exchange option in the chapter. What do these results suggest about the value of exchange options as a function of the correlation between the two assets?

We begin by computing intermediate values as follows:

$$\Sigma^2 = \sigma_1^2 + \sigma_2^2 - 2\rho\,\sigma_1\,\sigma_2$$

$$= 0.3\,(0.3) + 0.2\,(0.2) - 2\,(0.0)\,(0.3)\,(0.2)$$

$$= 0.13$$

$$w_1 = \frac{\ln\left(\dfrac{S_2}{S_1}\right) + (\delta_1 - \delta_2 + 0.5\,\Sigma^2)\,(T - t)}{\Sigma\sqrt{T - t}}$$

$$= \frac{\ln\left(\dfrac{100}{100}\right) + [0.05 - 0.05 + 0.5\,(0.13)]\,(0.5)}{\sqrt{0.13}\,\sqrt{0.5}}$$

$$= 0.127475$$

$$w_2 = \frac{\ln\left(\dfrac{S_2}{S_1}\right) + (\delta_1 - \delta_2 + 0.5\,\Sigma^2)\,(T - t)}{\Sigma\sqrt{T - t}} - \Sigma\sqrt{T - t}$$

$$= \frac{\ln\left(\dfrac{100}{100}\right) + [0.05 - 0.05 + 0.5\,(0.13)]\,(0.5)}{\sqrt{0.13}\,\sqrt{0.5}} - \sqrt{0.13}\,\sqrt{0.5}$$

$$=- \ -0.127475$$

With these values, $N(w_1) = 0.550718$, and $N(w_2) = 0.449282$. The valuation equation is:

$$EXOPT = S_2\,e^{-\delta_2\,(T - t)}\,N(w_1) - S_1\,e^{-\delta_1\,(T - t)}\,N(w_2)$$

$$EXOPT = 100\,e^{-0.05\,(0.5)}\,0.550718 - 100\,e^{-0.05\,(0.5)}\,0.449282$$

$$= 53.712072 - 43.818919$$

$$= 9.8932$$

We now compute the value of the same option with $\rho = 0.7$.

$$\Sigma^2 = \sigma_1^2 + \sigma_2^2 - 2\rho\,\sigma_1\,\sigma_2$$

$$= 0.3\,(0.3) + 0.2\,(0.2) - 2\,(0.7)\,(0.3)\,(0.2)$$

$$= 0.046$$

$$w_1 = \frac{\ln\left(\dfrac{S_2}{S_1}\right) + (\delta_1 - \delta_2 + 0.5\,\Sigma^2)\,(T - t)}{\Sigma\sqrt{T - t}}$$

$$= \frac{\ln\left(\dfrac{100}{100}\right) + [0.05 - 0.05 + 0.5\,(0.046]\,(0.5)}{\sqrt{0.046}\,\sqrt{0.5}}$$

$$= 0.075829$$

$$w_2 = \frac{\ln\left(\dfrac{S_2}{S_1}\right) + (\delta_1 - \delta_2 + 0.5\,\Sigma^2)\,(T - t)}{\Sigma\sqrt{T - t}} - \Sigma\sqrt{T - t}$$

$$= \frac{\ln\left(\dfrac{100}{100}\right) + [0.05 - 0.05 + 0.5\,(0.046)]\,(0.5)}{\sqrt{0.046}\,\sqrt{0.5}} - \sqrt{0.046}\,\sqrt{0.5}$$

$$= -0.075829$$

With these values, $N(w_1) = 0.530223$, and $N(w_2) = 0.469777$. Therefore,

$$EXOPT = 100\,e^{-0.05\,(0.5)}\,0.530223 - 100\,e^{-0.05\,(0.5)}\,0.469777$$

$$= 51.713175 - 45.817134$$

$$= 5.8960$$

For these parameter values, but differing correlations, we have values as follows: for $\rho = 0.0$, the price is 9.8932; for $\rho = 0.5$, the price is 7.2687 as shown in the text; and for $\rho = 0.7$, the price is 5.8960. Therefore, the price of the option varies inversely with the correlation.

For rainbow options, consider these parameter values: $S_1 = 100$; $S_2 = 100$; $X = 95$; $T - t = 0.5$ years; $\sigma_1 = 0.4$; $\sigma_2 = 0.5$; $r = 0.06$; $\delta_1 = 0.02$; $\delta_2 = 0.03$; and $\rho = 0.2$.(Interpret $X = 95$ as the exercise price or as the cash payment depending on the type of option.) Use this information for problems 12 - 18.

All of the following problems rely on some common values which we compute here and use in the specific solutions below.

$$\Sigma^2 = \sigma_1^2 + \sigma_2^2 - 2\rho\sigma_1\sigma_2 = 0.4(0.4) + 0.5(0.5) - 2(0.2)(0.4)(0.5) = 0.33$$

$$\rho_1 = \frac{\rho\sigma_2 - \sigma_1}{\Sigma} = \frac{0.2(0.5) - 0.4}{\sqrt{0.33}} = -0.522233$$

$$\rho_2 = \frac{\rho\sigma_1 - \sigma_2}{\Sigma} = \frac{0.2(0.4) - 0.5}{\sqrt{0.33}} = -0.731126$$

$$w_1 = \frac{\ln\left(\dfrac{S_1}{X}\right) + (r - \delta_1 + 0.5\sigma_1^2)(T - t)}{\sigma_1\sqrt{T - t}}$$

$$= \frac{\ln\left(\dfrac{100}{95}\right) + [0.06 - 0.02 + 0.5(0.4)(0.4)](0.5)}{0.4\sqrt{0.5}}$$

$$= 0.393481$$

$$w_2 = \frac{\ln\left(\dfrac{S_2}{X}\right) + [r - \delta_2 + 0.5\sigma_2^2](T - t)}{\sigma_2\sqrt{T - t}}$$

$$= \frac{\ln\left(\dfrac{100}{95}\right) + [0.06 - 0.03 + 0.5(0.5)(0.5)](0.5)}{0.5\sqrt{0.5}}$$

$$= 0.364282$$

$$w_3 = \frac{\ln\left(\dfrac{S_1}{S_2}\right) + (\delta_2 - \delta_1 + 0.5\,\Sigma^2)\,(T - t)}{\Sigma\sqrt{T - t}}$$

$$= \frac{\ln\left(\dfrac{100}{100}\right) + [0.03 - 0.02 + 0.5\,(0.33)\,]\,(0.5)}{\sqrt{0.33}\,\sqrt{0.5}}$$

$$= 0.215410$$

$$w_4 = \frac{\ln\left(\dfrac{S_2}{S_1}\right) + (\delta_1 - \delta_2 + 0.5\,\Sigma^2)\,(T - t)}{\Sigma\sqrt{T - t}}$$

$$= \frac{\ln\left(\dfrac{100}{100}\right) + [0.02 - 0.03 + 0.5\,(0.33)\,]\,(0.5)}{\sqrt{0.33}\,\sqrt{0.5}}$$

$$= 0.190792$$

The basic evaluation units that we require are:

$Q1.$ $S_1\,e^{-\delta_1(T-t)}\left\{\,N(w_3) - N_2(-w_1;\ w_3;\ \rho_1)\,\right\}$

$Q2.$ $S_2\,e^{-\delta_2(T-t)}\left\{\,N(w_4) - N_2(-w_2;\ w_4;\ \rho_2)\,\right\}$

$Q3.$ $X\,e^{-r(T-t)}\,N_2\left(-w_1 + \sigma_1\sqrt{T - t}\ ;\ -w_2 + \sigma_2\sqrt{T - t}\ ;\ \rho\right)$

To evaluate Q1–Q3, we need the following intermediate values:

$$S_1 e^{-\delta_1 (T - t)} = 100 \, e^{-0.02 \, (0.5)} = 99.004983$$

$$S_2 e^{-\delta_2 (T - t)} = 100 \, e^{-0.03 \, (0.5)} = 98.511194$$

$$X e^{-r (T - t)} = 95 \, e^{-0.06 \, (0.5)} = 92.192326$$

$$N(w_3) = N(0.215410) = 0.585276$$

$$N(w_4) = N(0.190792) = 0.575656$$

$$N_2 (-w_1; \, w_3; \, \rho_1) =$$

$$N_2 (-0.393481; \, 0.215410; \, -0.522233) = 0.122795$$

$$N_2 (-w_2; \, w_4; \, \rho_2) =$$

$$N_2 (-0.364282; \, 0.190792; \, -0.731126) = 0.084427$$

$$N_2 \left(-w_1 + \sigma_1 \sqrt{T - t} \; ; \; -w_2 + \sigma_2 \sqrt{T - t} \; ; \; \rho \right) =$$

$$N_2 \left(-0.393481 + 0.4 \sqrt{0.5} \; ; \; -0.364282 + 0.5 \sqrt{0.5} \; ; \; 0.2 \right) = 0.257875$$

Using the previous intermediate results, we now compute Q1-Q3:

$$Q1 = S_1 e^{-\delta_1 (T - t)} \left\{ N(w_3) - N_2 (-w_1; \, w_3; \, \rho_1) \right\}$$

$$= 99.004983 \, (0.585276 - 0.122795)$$

$$= 45.787924$$

$$Q2 = S_2 e^{-\delta_2 (T - t)} \left\{ N(w_4) - N_2 (-w_2; \, w_4; \, \rho_2) \right\}$$

$$= 98.511194 \, (0.575656 - 0.084427)$$

$$= 48.391555$$

$$Q3 = X e^{-r(T - t)} N_2\left(-w_1 + \sigma_1 \sqrt{T - t} \; ; \; -w_2 + \sigma_2 \sqrt{T - t} \; ; \; \rho\right)$$

$$= \; 92.192326 \; (0.257875)$$

$$= \; 23.774096$$

12. Find the value of an option on the best of two assets and cash.

$$\text{BEST3} = Q1 + Q2 + Q3 = 45.787924 + 48.391555 + 23.774096 = 117.9536$$

13. Find the value of an option on the better of two assets.

The valuation equation is, CBETTER = BEST3, given that X = 0. If X = 0, several values computed above must be adjusted. First, Q3 = 0. However, w_1 and w_2 both change as well. Each has X alone in its denominator, thus w_1 and w_2 are both infinite. These are important in the computation of the bivariate cumulative normal values. For present purposes, within the context of the unit normal distribution, let these variables be set equal to 10.0. As shown below, the large values of w_1 and w_2 force the bivariate probabilities to zero.

$$X e^{-r(T - t)} = 0 \, e^{-0.06 \, (0.5)} = 0.0$$

$$N_2 \, (-w_1; \; w_3; \; \rho_1) = N_2 \, (-10.0; \; 0.215410; \; -0.522233) = 0.0$$

$$N_2 \, (-w_2; \; w_4; \; \rho_2) = N_2 \, (-10.0; \; 0.190792; \; -0.731126) = 0.0$$

These affect the computation of Q1 and Q2 as follows:

$$Q1 = S_1 \, e^{-\delta_1 (T - t)} \left\{ N(w_3) - N_2 \, (-w_1; \; w_3; \; \rho_1) \right\}$$

$$= 99.004983 \, (0.585276 - 0.0)$$

$$= 57.945254$$

$$Q2 = S_2 \, e^{-\delta_2 (T - t)} \left\{ N(w_4) - N_2 \, (-w_2; \; w_4; \; \rho_2) \right\}$$

$$= 98.511194 \, (0.575656 - 0.0)$$

$$= 56.708521$$

Therefore, CBETTER = Q1 + Q2 + Q3 = 57.945254 + 56.708521 + 0 = 114.6538.

14. Find the value of a call on the maximum of two assets.

   CMAX = BEST3 -$Xe^{-r(T-t)}$ = Q1 + Q2 + Q3 - $Xe^{-r(T-t)}$ = 117.9536 - 92.192326 = 25.761249

15. Find the value of a put on the maximum of two assets.

   PMAX = CMAX - CBETTER + $Xe^{-r(T-t)}$ = 25.761249 - 114.6538 + 92.192326 = 3.2998

16. Find the value of a call on the minimum of two assets.

   CMIN = $C_t^M(S_1)$ + $C_t^M(S_2)$ - CMAX = 14.4949 + 16.7708 - 25.761249 = 5.504451

17. Find the value of a call on the worse of two assets.

   CWORSE = $C_t^M(S_1)$ + $C_t^M(S_2)$ - CBETTER, given that X = 0

   = 99.004983 + 98.511194 - 114.6538 = 82.8624

18. Find the value of a put on the minimum of two assets.

   PMIN = CMIN - CWORSE + $Xe^{-r(T-t)}$ = 5.504451 - 82.8624 + 92.192326 = 14.8344

19
The Swaps Market: Introduction

Answers to Questions and Problems

1. Explain the differences between a plain vanilla interest rate swap and a plain vanilla currency swap.

   In a plain vanilla interest rate swap, one party pays a fixed rate of interest based on a given nominal amount, while the second party pays a floating rate of interest based on the same nominal amount. No principal is exchanged in the agreement. In a plain vanilla foreign currency swap, there are three different sets of cash flows. First, at the initiation of the swap, the two parties actually do exchange cash. The entire motivation for the currency swap is the actual need for funds denominated in a different currency. This differs from the interest rate swap in which both parties deal in dollars and can pay the net amount. Second, the parties make periodic interest payments to each other during the life of the swap agreement. Third, at the termination of the swap, the parties again exchange the principal.

2. What are the two major kinds of swap facilitators? What is the key difference between the roles they play?

   They are swap brokers and swap bankers (swap dealers). The swap broker helps complete a swap by bringing counterparties together and perhaps by providing consulting services. The swap broker does not take a financial position in the transaction. By contrast, a swap banker or swap dealer will take a financial position to help the two parties complete their transaction.

3. Assume that you are a financial manager for a large commercial bank and that you expect short–term interest rates to rise more than the yield curve would suggest. Would you rather pay a fixed long–term rate and receive a floating short rate, or the other way around? Explain your reasoning.

   You would prefer to pay a fixed long–term rate and receive a floating short–term rate. The initial short term rate that you receive will merely be the spot rate that prevails today. However, if your hunch is correct, the short–term rate will rise more than the market expects, and you will then receive that higher rate. Because your payments are fixed, you will reap a profit from your insight.

4. Explain the role that the notional principal plays in understanding swap transactions. Why is this principal amount regarded as only notional? (Hint: What is the dictionary definition of "notional"?)

    In interest rate swaps, all of the cash flows are based on a notional or fictional amount. This is essentially a matter of convenience in helping to conceptualize the transaction. The entire contract could be stated without regard to the principal amount. One definition of "notional" is "existing in idea only."

5. Consider a plain vanilla interest rate swap. Explain how the practice of net payments works.

    In a typical interest rate swap, each party is scheduled to make payments to the other at certain dates. For the fixed payor, these amounts are certain, but the payments that the floating payor will have to make are unknown at the outset of the transaction. In each period, one party will owe a large amount to the other, depending on how interest rates have changed. Rather than make two payments, the party owing the greater amount simply pays the difference between the two obligations.

6. Assume that the yield curve is flat, that the swaps market is efficient, and that two equally creditworthy counterparties engage in an interest rate swap. Who should pay the higher rate, the party that pays a floating short–term rate or the party that pays a fixed long–term rate? Explain.

    They should pay the same. If the yield curve is flat, short–term rates equal long–term rates. Barring a change in rates, the two parties should pay the same amounts to each other in each period. If interest rates change, however, the payments will no longer be the same.

7. In a currency swap, counterparties exchange the same sums at the beginning and the end of the swap period. Explain how this practice relates to the custom of making interest payments during the life of the swap agreement.

    At the outset, the two parties exchange cash denominated in two currencies. Each party pays interest on the currency it receives from the other. Thus, the exchange of currencies is the basis for computing all of the interest payments that will be made over the life of the agreement.

8. Explain why a currency swap is also called an "exchange of borrowings."

    In a currency swap, both parties pay and both parties receive actual cash. Each has borrowed from the other, so they have exchanged borrowings.

9.   Assume that LIBOR stands today at 9 percent and the seven–year T–note rate is 10 percent. Establish an indication pricing schedule for a seven-year interest rate swap, assuming that the swap dealer must make a gross spread of 40 basis points.

     In this problem, the T–note rate is above LIBOR, indicating a strongly upward sloping yield curve. A customer may elect to either pay or receive LIBOR, which now stands at 9 percent. For the swap dealer to make a gross spread of 40 basis points, and assuming that the spread is set to be even around LIBOR, the swap dealer would be prepared to receive LIBOR and pay 8.80 percent. Alternative, if the swap dealer must pay LIBOR, he or she must receive 9.20. With the T–note rate at 10.00 percent, the swap dealer must be prepared to pay the T–note rate minus 120 basis points or to receive the T–note rate minus 80 basis points.

10.   Explain how basis risk affects a swap dealer. Does it affect a swap broker the same way? Explain.

      Basis risk affects a swap dealer because it changes the gross profit margin that the dealer will receive. For example, assume that a swap dealer agrees to pay LIBOR and receive the two–year T–note rate plus 60 basis points. This agreement is based upon a perception of the normal spread between LIBOR and the two–year T–note. This spread can change due to shifts in the term structure, but it can also change due to political disturbances or other causes. Basis risk arises from changes of the second kind. For example, political unrest in Europe might cause LIBOR to rise relative to U.S. rates. In our example, the dealer would have to pay a higher rate without receiving any correlatively higher rate. This problem does not affect the swap broker, because the swap broker does not take a risk position in the transaction.

11.   Assume a swap dealer attempts to function as a pure financial intermediary avoiding all interest rate risk. Explain how such a dealer may yet come to bear interest rate risk.

      A pure financial intermediary takes no risk position in the transactions it helps to consummate. In the real world, however, there are few things that are pure. A swap dealer might wish to avoid all risk positions, but some transactions will not be completed without the swap dealer's participation. This arises due to mismatches between the needs of two counterparties. In such a circumstance, the dealer faces two choices: take no risk position and allow the deal to fail or take a risk position to consummate the transaction. Thus, even risk averse swap dealers often find themselves with undesired risk positions that must be hedged away.

20
The Swaps Market: Refinements

Answers to Questions and Problems

1. What is the difference between a seasonal and a roller coaster swap?

    In a seasonal swap, the notional principal varies according to a fixed plan. When the swap has radically fluctuating and irregular notional principal amounts, the swap is called a roller coaster swap.

2. Compare and contrast an accreting and an amortizing swap.

    In an amortizing swap, the notional principal is reduced over time, while the notional principal in an accreting swap increases over time. Generally, these changes in notional principal occur on a schedule established when the swap agreement is negotiated.

3. Generally, political unrest in Europe is accompanied by an increase in the yield differential between Eurocurrency deposit rates and U.S. T–bill rates. Explain how to construct a basis swap to profit from such a development. Explain how this might be related to a TED spread in futures.

    In a basis swap, both parties make floating rate payments, but the payments are tied to different indexes. Thus, to exploit generally unexpected political turmoil in Europe, one might agree to pay based on U.S. T–bill rates and to receive based on Eurocurrency deposit rates. In a TED spread in the futures market, one trades a T–bill futures contract against a Eurodollar futures contract. In this specific case, a trader would sell the Eurodollar futures and buy the T–bill futures to exploit a widening yield differential.

4. Using interest rate swaps based on U.S. Treasury instruments, explain how to create a yield curve swap that will profit if the yield curve has an upward slope and the curve steepens. Explain how this might be related to the NOB spread in futures.

To profit from steepening yield curve, a trader could agree to receive floating payments based on the yield of a long–term instrument (such as a T–bond) and to make floating payments based on the yield of a short–term instrument (such as a T–bill). In the NOB trade in the futures market, a trader trades a T–note futures contract against a T–bond futures contract. Thus, to profit from a steepening yield curve, the trader would sell T–bond futures and buy T–note futures.

5. Explain how two foreign currency swaps might be combined to create a fixed–for–fixed foreign currency swap.

Two fixed–for–floating currency swaps can be combined to created a fixed–for–fixed swap. Assume that in one swap a firm pays floating payments in Currency A and receives fixed payments in Currency B. The firm also has a second swap in which it makes fixed payments in Currency C and receives floating payments in Currency A. Assuming that these two swaps have the same notional amount, the payments in Currency A offset each other. This leaves the firm receiving fixed payments in Currency B and making fixed payments in Currency A.

6. "An equity swap is nothing but a commodity swap!" Do you agree or disagree with this statement? Explain.

In essence, the statement is correct. A commodity swap involves one party making payments that are fixed relative to the price of a commodity and the other party making payments that float with the value of the underlying commodity. In an equity swap, the agreement has the same structure, except the underlying commodity may be thought of as a stock index or a stock portfolio.

7. Consider two interest rate swaps to pay fixed and receive floating. The two swaps require the same payments each semiannual period, but one swap has a tenor of five years, while the second has a tenor of ten years. Assume that you buy the ten–year swap and sell the five–year swap. What kind of instrument do these transactions create? Explain.

The net payment from these swaps during the first five years is zero, because the two exactly cancel each other. This leaves a long position in a swap that begins in five years with a tenor of five years. Thus, the resulting position is essentially a forward swap.

8. "A swaption is essentially a portfolio of options on futures or options on forwards." Is this statement correct? Explain.

This is false. A swaption is a single option on a swap agreement, not a portfolio of options. However, the swap agreement may be viewed as a portfolio of forward contracts.

9. Explain how an interest rate swap can be analyzed as a strip of futures.

We have already noted that a swap may be regarded as a portfolio of forward contracts. A swap may also be thought of as a portfolio of forward contracts. For example, a swap agreement with quarterly payments based on Eurodollar deposit rates is essentially similar to a strip of Eurodollar futures contracts in which the futures maturities match the payment dates on the swap.

10. Assume you can borrow at a fixed rate for ten years for 11 percent or that you can borrow at a floating rate of LIBOR plus 40 basis points for ten years. Assume also that LIBOR stands at 10.60 percent. Under these circumstances, your financial advisor states: "The all–in cost is the same on both deals—11 percent. Therefore, the two are equivalent and one should be indifferent between these two financing alternatives." How would you react? Explain.

Your financial advisor is naive, because she is neglecting the shape of the term–structure. Her advice would have some foundation if the yield curve were flat at 11 percent. In this situation, the expected cost on the two alternatives would be the same. However, the short–term strategy still involves risks (and opportunities) that the fixed rate strategy does not possess.

Solutions to Exercises for OPTION!

1. Consider a call and a put option on the same underlying stock. Both options have an exercise price of $75. The call costs $5, and the put costs $4. If you buy both the call and the put, what is the position called? Complete the following table showing the value and profits and losses at expiration. Complete an OPTION! graph showing both the value of the position at expiration and the profits and losses on the position at expiration.

Stock Price at Expiration	Position Value at Expiration	Position Profit at Expiration
$50	25.00	16.00
$65	10.00	1.00
$70	5.00	–4.00
$75	0.00	–9.00
$80	5.00	–4.00
$85	10.00	1.00
$90	15.00	6.00

Graph A for Problem 1

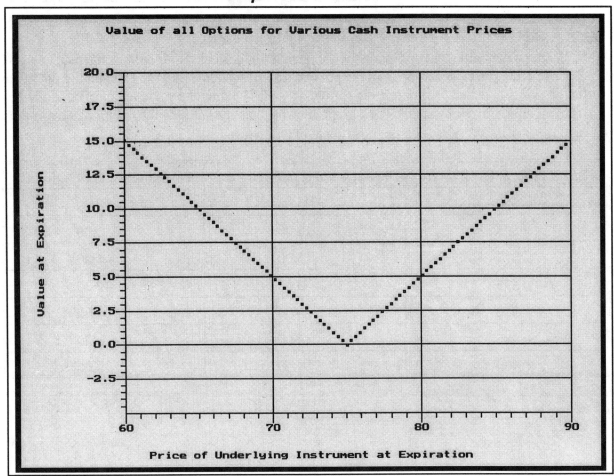

Value of all Options for Various Cash Instrument Prices

Graph B for Problem 1

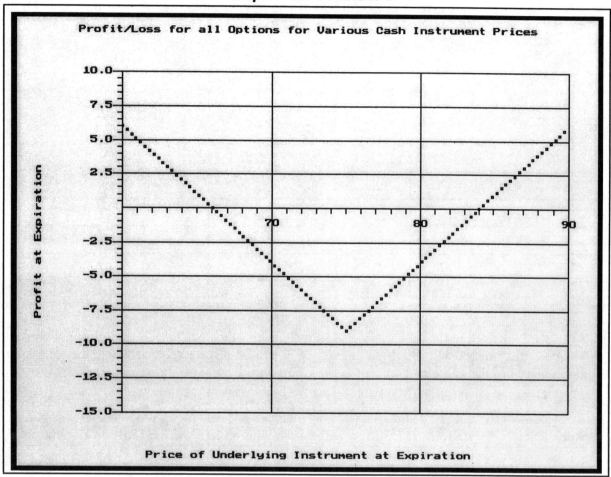

2. Consider a call and a put on the same underlying stock. Both options have the same exercise price of $50. The stock currently sells for $50. If you buy the stock, sell the put for $3, and buy the call for $4, complete following table showing the value of the entire position and the profits and losses on the position at expiration.

Stock Price at Expiration	Position Value at Expiration	Position Profit at Expiration
$35	20	−31
$40	30	−21
$45	40	−11
$50	50	−1
$55	60	9
$60	70	19
$65	80	29

3. Consider two calls on the same underlying stock. The calls have the same expiration date and exercise prices of $80 and $90. If the calls cost $12 and $4, respectively, complete the following table showing the value of and profits on a bull spread at expiration using these two calls. Prepare an OPTION! graph showing the profits and losses at expiration.

Stock Price at Expiration	Position Value at Expiration	Position Profit at Expiration
$70	0	−8
$75	0	−8
$80	0	−8
$85	5	−3
$90	10	2
$95	10	2
$100	10	2
$105	10	2
$110	10	2

Graph for Problem 3

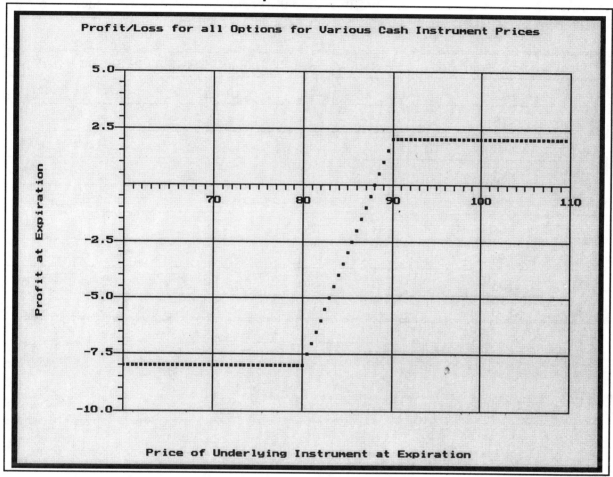

4. Consider two puts on the same underlying stock. The puts have the same expiration date and exercise prices of $80 and $90. If the puts cost $4 and $12, respectively, complete the following table showing the value of and profits on a bull spread at expiration using these two puts. Prepare an OPTION! graph showing the profits and losses at expiration.

Stock Price at Expiration	Position Value at Expiration	Position Profit at Expiration
$70	−10	−2
$75	−10	−2
$80	−10	−2
$85	−5	3
$90	0	8
$95	0	8
$100	0	8
$105	0	8
$110	0	8

Graph for Problem 4

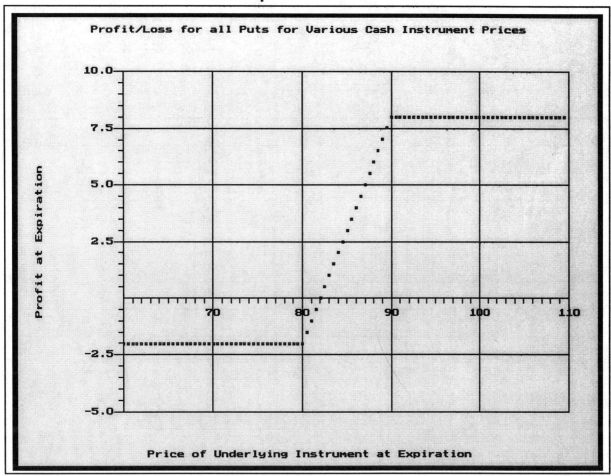

Profit/Loss for all Puts for Various Cash Instrument Prices

5. Consider two calls on the same underlying stock. The calls have the same expiration date and exercise prices of $80 and $90. If the calls cost $12 and $4, respectively, complete the following table showing the value of and profits on a bear spread at expiration using these two calls. Prepare an OPTION! graph showing the profits and losses at expiration.

Stock Price at Expiration	Position Value at Expiration	Position Profit at Expiration
$70	0	8
$75	0	8
$80	0	8
$85	−5	3
$90	−10	−2
$95	−10	−2
$100	−10	−2
$105	−10	−2
$110	−10	−2

Graph for Problem 5

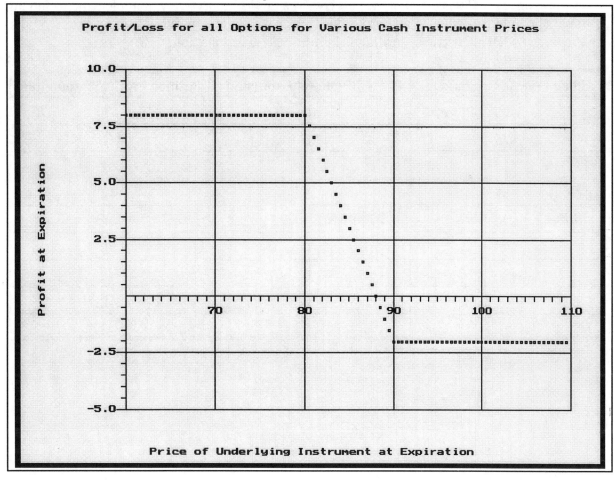

Profit/Loss for all Options for Various Cash Instrument Prices

Price of Underlying Instrument at Expiration

6. Consider two puts on the same underlying stock. The puts have the same expiration date and exercise prices of $80 and $90. If the puts cost $4 and $12, respectively, complete the following table showing the value of and profits on a bear spread at expiration using these two puts. Prepare an OPTION! graph showing the profits and losses at expiration.

Stock Price at Expiration	Position Value at Expiration	Position Profit at Expiration
$70	10	2
$75	10	2
$80	10	2
$85	5	−3
$90	0	−8
$95	0	−8
$100	0	−8
$105	0	−8
$110	0	−8

Graph for Problem 6

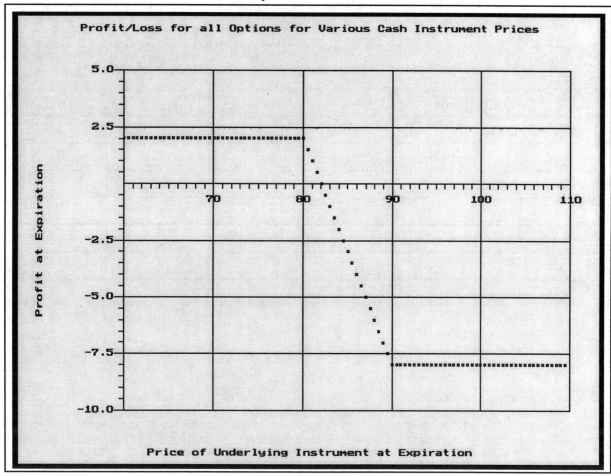

Profit/Loss for all Options for Various Cash Instrument Prices

7. For the same underlying stock, three calls with the same expiration date have exercise prices of $30, $35, and $40. For a long butterfly spread, complete the following table showing the value of and profits on the position at expiration. Prepare an OPTION! graph showing the profits and losses on the position at expiration assuming initial call prices of $11, $8, and $5 for the calls.

Stock Price at Expiration	Position Value at Expiration	Position Profit at Expiration
$20	0	0
$25	0	0
$30	0	0
$35	5	5
$40	0	0
$45	0	0
$50	0	0

Graph for Problem 7

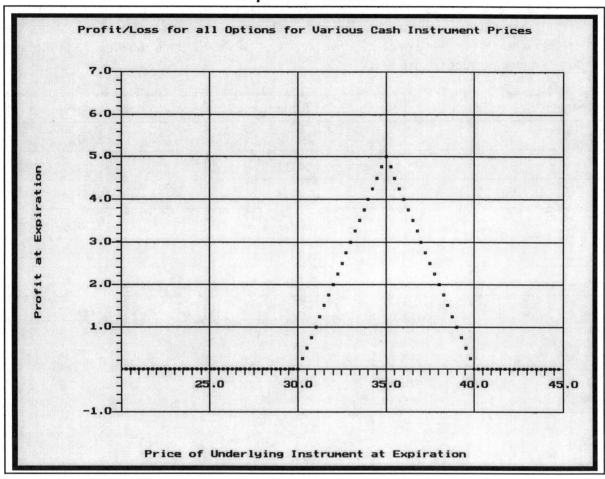

8. For the same underlying stock, two calls with the same expiration date have exercise prices of $30 and $40 and cost $11 and $8, respectively. Using these options, create two bull ratio spreads, one with a 2:1 ratio and the other with a 3:1 ratio. Complete the following table for the profits on the two spreads. For each spread, prepare an OPTION! graph showing the profits and losses on the positions at expiration.

Stock Price at Expiration	Profits on 2:1 Ratio Spread	Profits on 3:1 Ratio Spread
$20	−14.00	−25.00
$25	−14.00	−25.00
$30	−14.00	−25.00
$35	−4.00	−10.00
$40	6.00	5.00
$45	11.00	15.00
$50	16.00	25.00

Graph A for Problem 8

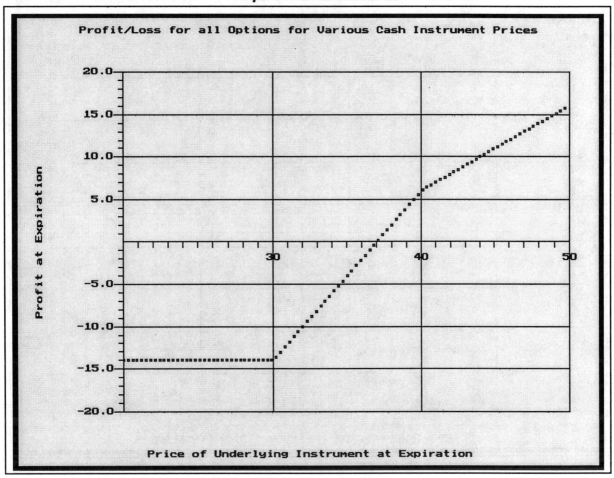

Profit/Loss for all Options for Various Cash Instrument Prices

Graph B for Problem 8

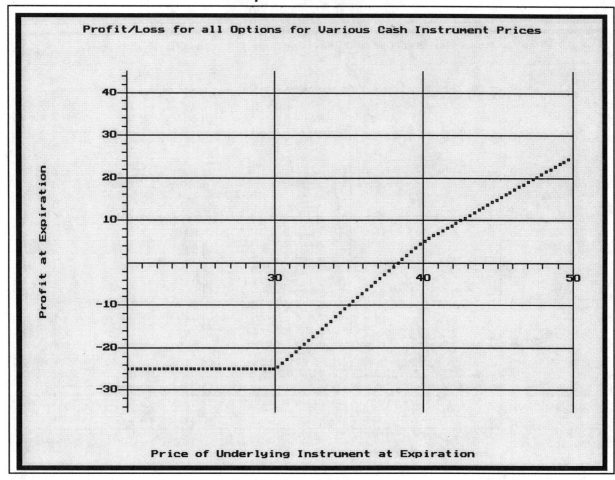

Profit/Loss for all Options for Various Cash Instrument Prices

Price of Underlying Instrument at Expiration

9. A stock now sells at $70 and a put on this stock with an exercise price of $70 costs $4. Using these instruments, create an insured portfolio and complete the following table.

Stock Price at Expiration	Profits on Stock Alone	Profits on Insured Portfolio
$50	–20	–4
$55	–15	–4
$60	–10	–4
$65	–5	–4
$70	0	–4
$75	5	1
$80	10	6
$85	15	11
$90	20	16

10. A stock sells at $100, and a call and a put on this stock both expire in one year and have the same exercise price of $100. The risk–free rate of interest is 9 percent. For a position that is long the call, short the stock, and long a bond that pays $100 in one year, complete the following table. What can you infer from the table?

Stock Price at Expiration	Value of Combined Position	Value of Call – Put
$80	20	–20
$85	15	–15
$90	10	–10
$95	5	–5
$100	0	0
$105	0	5
$110	0	10
$115	0	15
$120	0	20

The long call/short put portfolio in the last column has the same profit and loss profile as the stock alone. The combined position of the middle column (long call/short stock/long bond) has the same value profile as a put. This is reasonable, because from put–call parity, the combined position constitutes a synthetic put.

11. Consider a call option that expires in one year and has an exercise price of $100. The underlying stock price is $150, and the risk–free rate of interest is 10 percent. From these facts alone, what can you say about the current price of the call option? Using these values in the Black–Scholes model, complete the following table. Draw a graph showing the price of this call as a function of the standard deviation using the values in the table. What does this show about the no–arbitrage bounds for the price of a call option?

Standard Deviation	Call Price
.9	77.36
.8	73.80
.7	70.35
.6	67.10
.5	64.18
.4	61.78
.3	60.17
.2	59.56
.1	59.52
.01	59.52

Graph for Problem 11

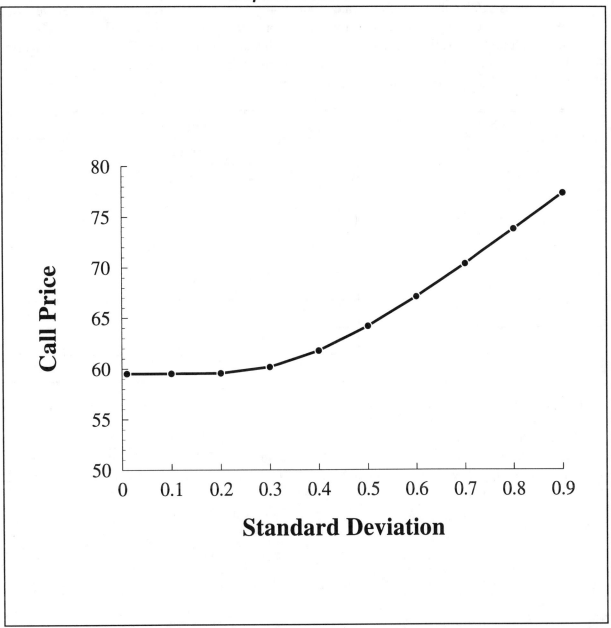

The price of a European call must always equal or exceed $S - X^{-r(T-\,)}$. For this option that quantity is \$59.52. Therefore, from the indicated facts alone, we know that the call price must be at least \$59.52. The table shows that the price of the call falls for lower values of the standard deviation. These values converge on \$59.52. Thus, the table and the accompanying graph show that value above this boundary is due to the volatility of the underlying good.

12. Consider a put option that expires in one year and has an exercise price of $150. The underlying stock price is $100, and the risk–free rate of interest is 10 percent. From these facts alone, what can you say about the current price of the put option? Using these values in the Black–Scholes model, complete the following table. Draw a graph showing the price of this put as a function of the standard deviation using the values in the table. What does this show about the no–arbitrage bounds for the price of a put option?

Standard Deviation	Put Price
.9	60.96
.8	56.98
.7	52.99
.6	49.05
.5	45.22
.4	41.63
.3	38.52
.2	36.36
.1	35.73
.01	35.73

For a European put, the lower bound of value is $Xe^{-r(T-t)} - S$. For these values, this bound is $35.73, so the put price must equal or exceed this amount. As the standard deviation falls, the value of the put converges to this bound of $35.73. Therefore, any excess value above $35.73 is due to the volatility of the underlying good.

Graph for Problem 12

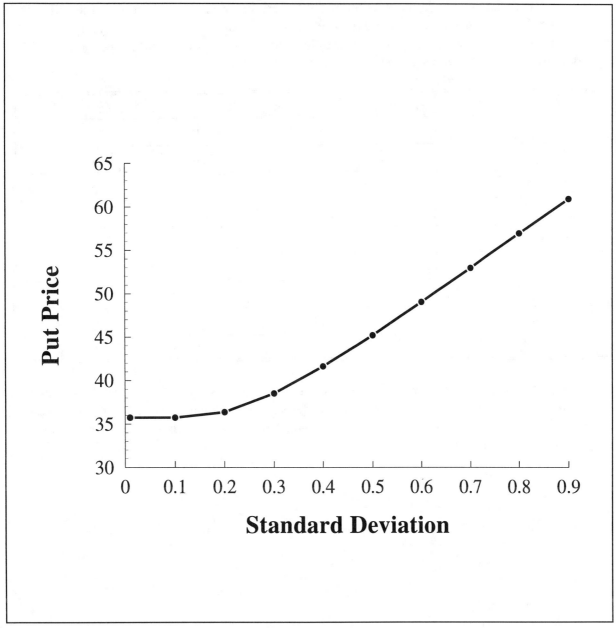

13. A put option has an exercise price of $100 and expires in one year. The risk–free rate of interest is 10 percent, and the standard deviation of the underlying stock is .2. Complete the following table. Explain what the table shows about the value of European versus American put options. Prepare a graph showing the put price and the intrinsic value of the put as a function of the stock price using the values in the table below.

Stock Price	Black–Scholes European Put Price	Intrinsic Value of Put
$80	13.27	20
$85	10.07	15
$90	7.43	10
$95	5.35	5
$100	3.75	0
$105	2.58	0
$110	1.73	0
$115	1.11	0
$120	.74	0

For puts deep–in–the–money, the price is less than the intrinsic value, because the put owner cannot exercise and obtain the intrinsic value. Rather, the put's value approximates the present value of the intrinsic value. For puts near–the–money or deep–in–the–money, the put's value exceeds the intrinsic value.

Graph for Problem 13

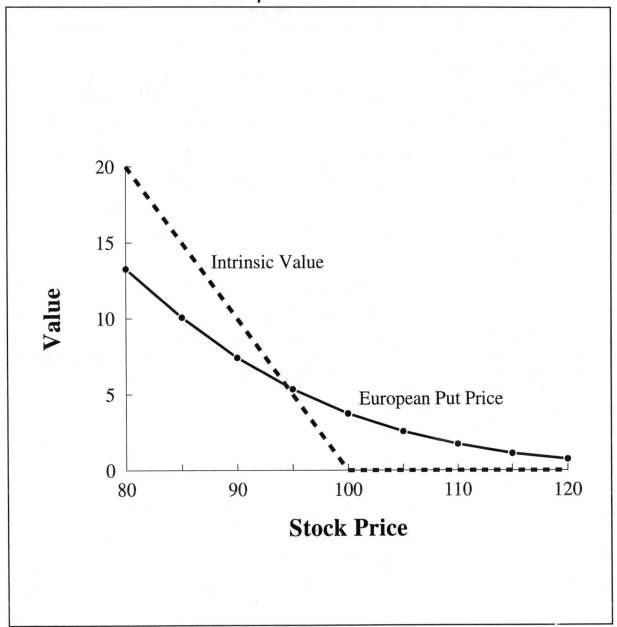

14. A put option has an exercise price of $100 and the underlying stock is worth $80. The risk–free rate of interest is 10 percent, and the standard deviation of the underlying stock is .2. Complete the following table. Explain what the table shows about the value of European versus American put options.

Days Until Expiration	Black–Scholes European Put Price	Intrinsic Value of Put
5	19.86	20
10	19.73	20
30	19.18	20
90	17.64	20
180	15.82	20
270	14.45	20
365	13.27	20

We know that the value of an American option must always equal or exceed its intrinsic value, so the American put price must always equal or exceed $20 in this example. For this deep–in–the–money European put, the price is near the intrinsic value with little time until expiration. However, when considerable time remains until expiration, the European put price is well below the intrinsic value.

15. Consider two call options on the same underlying stock. The calls have exercise prices of $80 and $90 and both expire in 150 days. The risk–free rate of interest is 8 percent, and the stock price is $100. Using the Black–Scholes model, complete the following table. What principle does the table illustrate regarding boundary conditions on call options?

Standard Deviation	Call Price $X = \$80$	Call Price $X = \$90$	Price Difference
.9	33.32	28.28	5.04
.8	31.38	26.05	5.33
.7	29.48	23.83	5.65
.6	27.66	21.62	6.04
.5	25.96	19.45	6.51
.4	24.46	17.34	7.12
.3	23.31	15.39	7.92
.2	22.68	13.77	8.91
.1	22.59	12.94	9.65
.01	22.59	12.91	9.68

As a no–arbitrage condition, the price difference between two calls on the same underlying good with the same expiration date can never exceed the difference in the two exercise prices. For the options in this problem, that difference is $10.00. As the table indicates, the price differential approaches the difference in the exercise prices as the standard deviation falls. With a standard deviation of .01, the price difference is $9.68. Even more exactly, we might note that both options approach the boundary price of $S - Xe^{-r(T-t)}$. Therefore, we know that the price differential must approach $(X_{90} - X_{80})e^{-r(T-t)} = \$10e^{-.08(150/365)} = \$9.68$.

16. Consider a call option with an exercise price of $80 that expires in 150 days. The risk–free rate of interest is 8 percent, and the stock price is $80. Using the Black–Scholes model, complete the following table. What principle does the table illustrate regarding the pricing of call options? Prepare a graph using the data in the table expressing the value of the call option as a function of the standard deviation.

Standard Deviation	Call Price
.9	19.19
.8	17.25
.7	15.30
.6	13.34
.5	11.37
.4	9.39
.3	7.41
.2	5.45
.1	3.57
.01	2.59

For an at–the–money call, the call price varies directly with the standard deviation of the underlying good. This principle holds for all calls regardless of their moneyness.

Graph for Problem 16

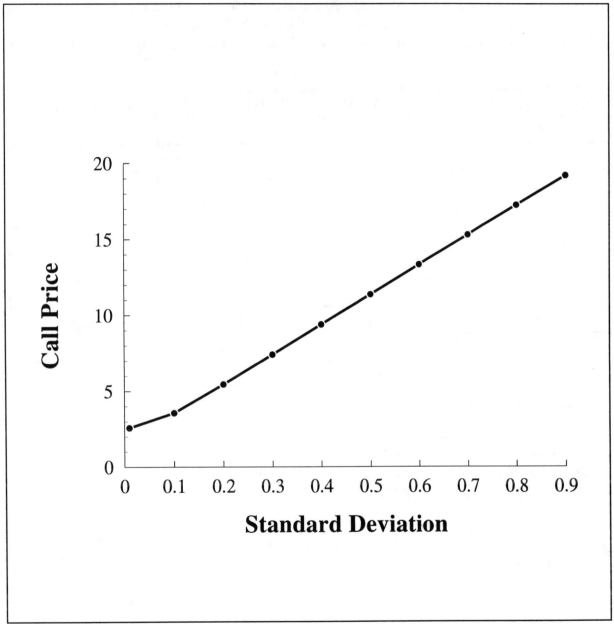

17. Consider two put options on the same underlying stock, with a standard deviation of .3. The puts have exercise prices of $80 and $90 and both expire in 150 days. The risk–free rate of interest is 8 percent, and the stock price is $60. Using the Black–Scholes model, complete the following table. What principle does the table illustrate regarding boundary conditions on put options?

Standard Deviation	Put Price $X = \$80$	Put Price $X = \$90$	Price Difference
.9	25.75	33.47	7.72
.8	24.25	32.06	7.81
.7	22.77	30.73	7.96
.6	21.36	29.52	8.16
.5	20.04	28.48	8.44
.4	18.88	27.69	8.81
.3	17.98	27.23	9.25
.2	17.49	27.09	9.60
.1	17.41	27.09	9.68
.01	17.41	27.09	9.68

The lower bound for a European put price is $Xe^{-r(T-t)} - S$, and the lower bound for the price difference between two European puts is the present value of the differences in the exercise prices. For our example, this is $\$10e^{-.08(150/365)} = \$9.68$. As the standard deviation becomes small, the options tend to their boundary price and the difference in prices tends to the present value of the difference in exercise prices of $9.68.

18. Consider two put options on the same underlying stock. The stock trades for $100. One put has an exercise price of $80, while the other has an exercise price of $120. The standard deviation of the stock is .3, and the risk–free rate of interest is 11 percent. Complete the following table. What does the completed table indicate about the influence of the time until expiration on the pricing of puts? Explain the difference in the price patterns for the two puts. Would call options exhibit the same kind of price pattern? Explain.

Days Until Expiration	Put Price $X = \$80$	Put Price $X = \$120$
100	.31	17.93
120	.43	17.77
140	.56	17.63
160	.68	17.51
180	.80	17.39
200	.92	17.28
220	1.03	17.18
240	1.14	17.08
260	1.24	16.98

Assuming that we are dealing with European puts, for the at–the–money put ($X = \$80$), the put price is larger the longer the time remaining until expiration. Because it is at–the–money, there is no intrinsic value to consider. For the deep–in–the–money put, with ($X = \$120$), the price is lower the longer the term until expiration. The more time remaining until expiration, the longer the put owner must wait to capture the intrinsic value of the option. This outweighs the general benefit of an option being more valuable the longer the term until expiration.

19. A call option expires in one period and has an exercise price of $100. The underlying stock price is also $100. The stock price can rise or fall by 10 percent over the period. Using the one–period binomial model, complete the following table. How is the probability of a stock price increase related to the interest rate? Explain why this relationship makes sense. Explain why the call price varies with the interest rate as it does.

Interest Rate	Call Price	Probability of a Stock Price Increase
0.01	5.45	.55
0.02	5.88	.60
0.03	6.31	.65
0.04	6.73	.70
0.05	7.14	.75
0.06	7.55	.80
0.07	7.94	.85
0.08	8.33	.90
0.09	8.72	.95

The interest rate indicates the risk–free rate of return available in the economy. To warrant the risk of holding an option, the expected return must be higher than this risk–free rate. If the stock price can rise by only 10 percent, then an ever higher interest rate must require a greater probability of achieving the 10 percent jump in the stock price. If it did not, the expected return from holding the option would not equal the risk–free rate and the central criterion of a risk–neutral economy would be violated.

20. A stock currently trades at $140 and a call option on the stock has an exercise price of $150 and expires in one year. The standard deviation of the stock price is .3, and the risk–free rate of interest is 12 percent. What is the Black–Scholes price for this call option? Complete the following table using the multi–period binomial model. What is the relationship between prices from the binomial model and the Black– Scholes model? Explain.

Periods	Binomial Model Price
1	21.95
2	19.88
5	20.13
10	20.24
25	19.88
50	19.99
100	19.98
150	20.01
200	20.00

The Black–Scholes price is $19.99. As the number of periods increases, the binomial model price becomes virtually identical with the Black–Scholes price. This makes sense, because the Black–Scholes model assumes infinitely small periods by its continuous time framework. As the number of periods in the binomial model increases, the period length becomes smaller. This gives an improved approximation to the Black–Scholes framework.

21. A stock currently trades at $140 and a call option on the stock has an exercise price of $150 and expires in one year. The call price is $11.00, and the risk–free rate of interest is 12 percent. What is the standard deviation of the underlying stock? Complete the following table using the Black–Scholes model to find each price, and show the price to four decimals. What does the completed table show about the technique necessary to find the volatility when the other parameters are known?

Standard Deviation	Call Price	Error
0.01	6.96	–4.04
0.2	14.71	3.71
0.1	9.62	–1.38
0.15	12.11	1.11
0.125	10.84	–0.16
0.13	11.09	0.09
0.1275	10.97	–0.03
0.1285	11.02	0.02
0.1282	11.00	0.00

The standard deviation of the underlying stock is 0.128133. The table illustrates an iterative search for the implied standard deviation. The table illustrates the method of bisection—the next guess of the standard deviation is half way between the two previous guesses. There are other fancier and more efficient search techniques available.

22. A stock trades for $75 and is expected to pay a dividend of $2 in 30 days. European call and put options on this stock expire in 90 days and have an exercise price of $75. The risk–free rate of interest is 7 percent, and the standard deviation of the stock is .3. Find the price of these options according to the Black–Scholes model, ignoring dividends. What are the values of these European options according to the adjustments to the Black–Scholes model for known dividends? Verify your answer by showing your own calculations.

    The call is worth $4.01 and the put is worth $4.72.

23. A stock trades at $40 and has a standard deviation of .4. The risk–free rate is 8 percent. A European call and put on this stock expire in 90 days. The exercise price for the call is $35, and the exercise price for the put is $45. Using the Merton model, complete the following table. What does the completed table show about the influence of dividends on call and put prices?

Continuous Dividend Rate	Call Price	Put Price
0.005	6.57	5.82
0.01	6.53	5.85
0.02	6.45	5.91
0.03	6.37	5.98
0.05	6.22	6.11
0.075	6.03	6.27
0.1	5.84	6.44
0.125	5.66	6.61
0.15	5.48	6.78

Other factors held constant, an increasing dividend rate causes call prices to fall and put prices to rise.

24. A stock pays a continuous dividend of 3 percent and currently sells for $80. The risk–free rate of interest is 7 percent, and the standard deviation on the stock is .25. A European call and put on this stock both have an exercise price of $75 and expire in 180 days. Find the price of these options according to the Black–Scholes model (i.e., ignoring the dividend) and the Merton model. Find the price of these options according to the binomial model with 5, 25, 50, 100, and 200 periods.

    Ignoring dividends, the Black–Scholes call and put prices are $9.93 and $2.38, respectively. The Merton call and put prices are $9.07 and $2.70, respectively. The following table shows the binomial call and put prices.

Periods	Call Price	Put Price
5	9.00	2.63
25	9.11	2.82
50	9.09	2.72
100	9.07	2.70
200	9.08	2.71

25. A stock pays a proportional dividend equal to 2 percent of its value in 150 days. The current stock price is $120, the risk–free rate is 9 percent, and the standard deviation of the stock is .2. A European call and put option on this stock both expire in 270 days and both have an exercise price of $120. Find the price of these options according to the Black–Scholes model (i.e., ignoring the dividend) and the Merton model. Find the price of these options according to the binomial model with 5, 25, 50, 100, and 200 periods.

    The Black–Scholes call and put prices are $8.45 and $4.09, respectively. The Merton call and put prices are $7.83 and $4.46, respectively.

Periods	Call Price	Put Price
5	8.12	4.74
25	7.89	4.52
50	7.80	4.43
100	7.82	4.44
200	7.83	4.45

26. A stock will pay a cash dividend of $1.75 in 150 days. The current stock price is $120, the risk–free rate is 9 percent, and the standard deviation of the stock is .2. A European call and put option on this stock both expire in 270 days and both have an exercise price of $120. Find the price of these options according to the Black– Scholes model (i.e., ignoring the dividend) and the Merton model. Find the price of these options according to the binomial model with 5, 25, 50, 100, and 200 periods.

The Black–Scholes call and put prices are $12.41 and $4.68, respectively. A dividend of $1.75 in 150 days is at a rate of $4.26 per year on a stock with a current price of $120. This implies a continuous dividend rate of $\delta = 0.0355$. The Merton call and put prices are $10.38 and $5.76, respectively.

Periods	Call Price	Put Price
5	11.56	5.52
25	11.32	5.99
50	11.31	5.99
100	11.30	5.98
200	11.29	5.98

27. A stock trades at $80 and has a standard deviation of .4. The risk–free rate of interest is 6 percent. A European call and put both expire in 100 days and have the same exercise price of $80. Complete the following table for the sensitivities of the two options.

Call					
Stock	DELTA	THETA	VEGA	RHO	GAMMA
$60	.1169	−4.8821	6.1656	1.7405	.0156
$65	.2094	−7.8745	9.7886	3.3281	.0211
$70	.3247	−10.8194	13.1823	5.4626	.0245
$75	.4502	−13.0861	15.5392	7.9565	.0252
$80	.5727	−14.3025	16.4273	10.5551	.0234
$85	.6818	−14.4384	15.8727	13.0198	.0200
$90	.7721	−13.7135	14.2311	15.1819	.0160
$95	.8423	−12.4623	11.9840	16.9591	.0121
$100	.8942	−11.0048	9.5724	18.3424	.0087

Put					
Stock	DELTA	THETA	VEGA	RHO	GAMMA
$60	−.8831	−.1603	6.1656	−19.8200	.0156
$65	−.7906	−3.1528	9.7886	−18.2324	.0211
$70	−.6753	−6.0976	13.1823	−16.0979	.0245
$75	−.5498	−8.3644	15.5392	−13.6040	.0252
$80	−.4273	−9.5818	16.4273	−11.0053	.0234
$85	−.3182	−9.7167	15.8727	−8.5407	.0200
$90	−.2279	−8.9918	14.2311	−6.3785	.0160
$95	−.1577	−7.7406	11.9840	−4.6013	.0121
$100	−.1058	−6.2831	9.5724	−3.2181	.0087

28. A stock trades at $80 and has a standard deviation of .4. The stock pays a continuous dividend of 3 percent. The risk–free rate of interest is 6 percent. A European call and put both expire in 100 days and have the same exercise price of $80. Complete the following table for the sensitivities of the two options.

Call					
Stock	DELTA	THETA	VEGA	RHO	GAMMA
$60	.1084	−4.4159	5.8314	1.6172	.0148
$65	.1967	−7.1627	9.3979	3.1310	.0203
$70	.3082	−9.8589	12.8332	5.1953	.0239
$75	.4312	−11.8899	15.3247	7.6393	.0249
$80	.5527	−12.8817	16.3978	10.2179	.0234
$85	.6622	−12.7894	16.0253	12.6920	.0202
$90	.7538	−11.8264	14.5227	14.8865	.0164
$95	.8258	−10.3242	12.3542	16.7091	.0125
$100	.8795	−8.6077	9.9635	18.1417	.0091

Put					
Stock	DELTA	THETA	VEGA	RHO	GAMMA
$60	−.8834	−1.4794	5.8314	−19.9432	.0148
$65	−.7952	−4.3750	9.3979	−18.4295	.0203
$70	−.6836	−7.2199	12.8332	−16.3652	.0239
$75	−.5606	−9.3997	15.3247	−13.9211	.0249
$80	−.4391	−10.5403	16.3978	−11.3426	.0234
$85	−.3296	−10.5968	16.0253	−8.8684	.0202
$90	−.2380	−9.7825	14.5227	−6.6740	.0164
$95	−.1660	−8.4291	12.3542	−4.8514	.0125
$100	−.1123	−6.8614	9.9635	−3.4188	.0091

29. Two stocks have the same standard deviation of .4, but Stock A is priced at $110, and Stock B trades for $100. The risk–free rate is 11 percent. Consider two call options written on these two stocks that both expire in 90 days. Call A has an exercise price of $110, while Call B has an exercise price of $100. Find the DELTAs for these two options. What is unusual about the result, and how can it be explained?

The DELTAs for both options is .5932. They are identical because the DELTA depends only on the ratio of the stock price to the exercise price, not the stock and exercise prices in isolation. This is clear from considering the formula for d_1, which includes the ratio S/X.

30. A stock trades for $50 and has a standard deviation of .4. A call on the stock has an exercise price of $40 and expires in 55 days. The risk–free rate is 8 percent. Find the DELTA for the call, and explain how to create a delta–neutral portfolio. (Assume that you are short one call.) Complete the following table.

The DELTA is .9444. If we are to be short one call, the delta–neutral portfolio will consist of the short call plus a long position in the stock of .9444 shares.

Stock Price	Call Price	Portfolio Value
$45	6.22	36.28
$46	7.05	36.39
$47	7.92	36.47
$48	8.82	36.51
$49	9.74	36.54
$50	10.67	36.55
$51	11.63	36.53
$52	12.59	36.52
$53	13.56	36.49
$54	14.54	36.46
$55	15.52	36.42

31. A stock trades for $50 and has a standard deviation of .4. A call on the stock has an exercise price of $40 and expires in 55 days. The risk–free rate is 8 percent. Find the DELTA for the call, and explain how to create a delta–neutral portfolio. (Assume that you are short one call.) Complete the following table showing how the value of the delta–neutral portfolio changes over time. Assume the stock price does not change. How do you account for the change in the value of the delta–neutral portfolio?

The DELTA is .9444. A delta–neutral portfolio that is short one call must be long DELTA shares, or .9444 shares, in this problem. While the portfolio is delta–neutral when created at day 55, it does not remain delta–neutral over time. Specifically, the price of the call must decay to its intrinsic value of $10 by expiration. This is reflected in the table. Therefore, the value of the portfolio must change.

Days Until Expiration	Call Price	Portfolio Value
55	10.67	36.55
50	10.60	36.62
45	10.52	36.70
40	10.44	36.78
35	10.37	36.85
30	10.31	36.91
25	10.24	36.98
20	10.19	37.03
15	10.13	37.09
10	10.09	37.13
5	10.04	37.18

32. A stock trades for $100 and has a standard deviation of .3. A call on the stock has an exercise price of $100 and expires in 77 days. The risk–free rate is 8 percent. Find the DELTA for the call, and form a delta–neutral portfolio assuming that you are short one call. What is the GAMMA for the stock and for the call? Does the portfolio have a positive or negative GAMMA? Complete the following table. How do these values illustrate the GAMMA of the portfolio?

The DELTA is .5759 and the GAMMA is .0284. The delta–neutral portfolio consists of the short call plus a long position of .5759 shares. The GAMMA for the stock is zero, so the portfolio will have a GAMMA of –.0284, reflecting the short position in the call. The values in the table reflect the negative GAMMA of the portfolio because the portfolio value decreases at stock prices away from $100, the price used to establish the delta–neutral portfolio.

Stock Price	Call Price	Portfolio Value
$80	.36	45.71
$85	.94	48.01
$90	2.04	49.79
$95	3.81	50.90
$100	6.32	51.27
$105	9.54	50.93
$110	13.35	50.00
$115	17.61	48.62
$120	22.17	46.94

33. A stock with a standard deviation of .5 now trades for $100. Two calls on this stock both expire in 70 days and have exercise prices of $90 and $100. The risk–free rate is 10 percent. Find the DELTA and GAMMA for both calls. Construct a portfolio that is long one share of stock and that is both delta–neutral and gamma–neutral. For the portfolio, complete the following table.

For the call with $X = \$90$, the DELTA is .7512 and the GAMMA is .0145. For the call with $X = \$100$, the DELTA is .5781 and the GAMMA is .0179. Recalling that the DELTA of a stock is 1.0 and the GAMMA of a stock is zero, and letting N_{90} and N_{100} be the number of calls with $X = \$90$ and $X = \$100$, respectively, a delta–neutral and gamma–neutral portfolio must meet the following two conditions:

delta–neutrality $1 + .7512N_{90} + .5781N_{100} = 0$
gamma–neutrality $.0145N_{90} + .0179N_{100} = 0$

Solving these two equations for two unknowns gives $N_{90} = -3.5350$ and $N_{100} = 2.8637$. Therefore, the delta–neutral and gamma–neutral portfolio will consist of: long 1 share, short 3.5350 calls with $X = \$90$, and long 2.8637 calls with $X = \$100$. At a stock price of $100, the two calls are worth $15.35 and $9.62, so the entire portfolio costs:

$$\$100 - 3.5350(\$15.35) + 2.8637(\$9.62) = \$73.29, \text{ when } \sigma = .5.$$

Standard Deviation	Portfolio Value
.3	72.34
.35	72.82
.45	73.23
.5	73.29
.55	73.25
.6	73.16
.65	73.01
.7	72.83

34. A stock sells for $70, has a standard deviation of .3, and pays a 2 percent continuous dividend. The risk–free rate is 11 percent. Three calls on this stock all expire in 100 days and have exercise prices of $65, $70, and $75. Using these calls, construct a long position in a butterfly spread. What does the spread cost? Complete the following table for the profitability of the spread as a function of the stock price for the current time and for the expiration date. For the long position, is time decay beneficial or detrimental? Explain.

The three options cost $8.22, $5.20, and $3.05, for the $65, $70, and $75 exercise prices, respectively. Therefore, the spread, which is long one $65 call, short two $70 calls, and long one $75 call, costs $.87. Time decay is beneficial. If the stock price remains at $70, the value of the spread will go to $5.00 at expiration.

Stock Price	Profit with $T - t = 100$	Profit at Expiration
$50	−.76	−.87
$55	−.57	−.87
$60	−.28	−.87
$65	−.06	−.87
$70	.00	4.13
$75	−.11	−.87
$80	−.31	−.87
$85	−.51	−.87
$90	−.65	−.87

35. Consider a long position in a straddle with an exercise price of $50. The stock price is $80, and the standard deviation of the stock is .4. The risk–free rate is 6 percent, and the options expire in 180 days. What is the current price of the two options? Prepare a graph of the current value of the straddle as a function of the stock price. On the same axes, graph the value of the straddle at expiration. Let the range of stock prices range from $30 to $70. As a first step to preparing the graph, complete the following table.

The call is worth $31.72 and the put is worth $.26.

Stock Price	Current Straddle Price	Straddle Price at Expiration
$30	18.92	20.00
$35	14.93	15.00
$40	12.12	10.00
$45	10.82	5.00
$50	11.06	0.00
$55	12.68	5.00
$60	15.38	10.00
$65	18.88	15.00
$70	22.93	20.00

Graph for Problem 35

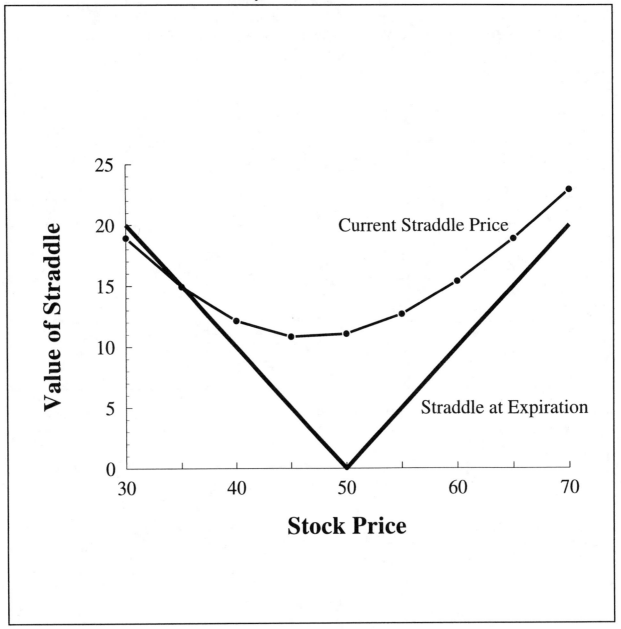

36. A stock trades at $50 and has a standard deviation of .3. The risk–free rate is 7 percent. An American and a European call on this stock both have an exercise price of $55, and both expire in 100 days. The stock will pay a dividend in 50 days, but the amount is uncertain. For the different possible dividend amounts shown in the table below, compute the exact American option price and the Black–Scholes model price with the known dividend adjustment. What kind of systematic difference do you notice in the pricing from the two models, if any?

Dividend Amount	Exact American	Black–Scholes Adjusted for Known Dividends
$.01	1.65	1.65
$.05	1.63	1.63
$.10	1.62	1.62
$.25	1.57	1.57
$.50	1.48	1.49
$1.00	1.34	1.33
$1.50	1.21	1.19
$2.00	1.10	1.06
$3.00	.93	.83

When the dividend is small relative to the value of the stock, the two models give the same answer to the penny. As the dividend becomes large relative to the stock price, the exact American price exceeds the Black–Scholes price adjusted for known dividends. This difference reflects the difference between American and European options, because as the dividend becomes larger, the early exercise privilege of an American option begins to have value.

37. A stock trades for $150 and has a standard deviation of .4. The risk–free rate of interest is 7 percent. Two dividends are expected. The first, due in 30 days, is for $1.50, while the second, due in 150 days, is $2.00. Find the pseudo–American option price for a call that expires in 200 days with an exercise price of $140. Also, find the option price according to the Black–Scholes model adjusted for known dividends.

The pseudo–American price is $23.13, and the Black–Scholes price adjusted for known dividends is also $23.13.

38. A stock with a standard deviation of .33 trades for $75. The risk–free rate is 6 percent. The stock pays a continuous dividend of 2 percent. An American call and put on this stock have an exercise price of $70 and both expire in 100 days. Find the price of these options using the

analytic approximation of the American option price. What are the critical values for the call and the put? Using the Merton model, find the price of both options.

The Merton model price for the call is $8.32, and for the put the price is $2.59. The analytic approximation gives a price of $8.32 for the call and $2.62 for the put. The critical price for the call is $237.23, while the critical price for the put is $53.39. The European and American call prices are the same (to the penny), because the current price of $75 is so far from the critical price for the call of $237.23. Therefore, the early exercise privilege of the American option has virtually no value.

39. A stock has a current price of $80 and a standard deviation of .3. The stock pays a continuous dividend of 3 percent. The risk–free rate is 7 percent. An American and a European call on this stock both expire in 200 days, and both have an exercise price of $70. Find the price of the American call according to the analytic approximation formula, and find the price of the European option according to the Merton model. What is the critical price for the American call? Complete the following table for the two options using the two respective models. Graph the price of the two options as a function of the stock price over the range from $60 to $100. Explain any particularly important features of the graph.

According to both the Merton model and the analytic approximation, the price is $13.63. The critical price for the call is $191.02.

Stock Price	American Call According to the Analytic Approximation	European Call According to the Merton Model
$60	2.37	2.37
$65	4.25	4.25
$70	6.80	6.80
$75	9.96	9.96
$80	13.63	13.63
$85	17.71	17.70
$90	22.07	22.07
$95	26.64	26.63
$100	31.34	31.33

The critical price for the call is $191.02. The graphs are virtually identical as the stock price is so far from the critical price and the early exercise feature has virtually no value. Only for stock prices above $90 does a difference in option values begin to emerge.

Graph for Problem 39

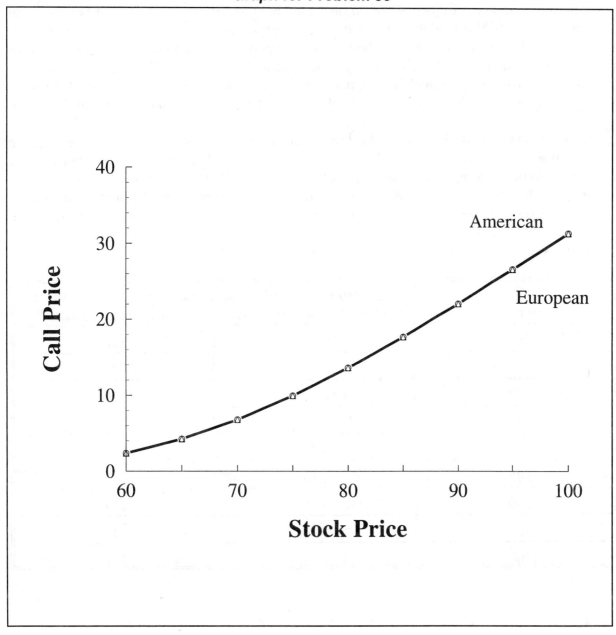

40. A stock has a current price of $70 and a standard deviation of .3. The risk–free rate is 7 percent. An American and a European put on this stock both expire in 200 days, and both have an exercise price of $80. Find the price of the American put according to the analytic approximation formula, and find the price of the European option according to the Merton model. What is the critical price for the American put? Complete the following table for the two options using the two respective models. Graph the price of the two options as a function of the stock price over the range from $60 to $100. Explain any particularly important features of the graph.

The put price according to the Merton model is $11.31 and according to the analytic approximation the price is $11.76. The critical price is $59.22. The American put is worth more than its intrinsic value in all instances shown in the table, while that is not true for the European put. Further, the price of the American put tends to its intrinsic value from above as the put becomes deep–in–the–money. For example, with a stock price of $60, the intrinsic value of the put is $20.00 and the value of the American put is $20.01. The price of the European put is often below its intrinsic value, due to the inability of exercise.

Stock Price	American Put According to the Analytic Approximation	European Put According to the Merton Model
$60	20.01	18.81
$65	15.52	14.80
$70	11.76	11.31
$75	8.68	8.39
$80	6.25	6.06
$85	4.40	4.27
$90	3.03	2.94
$95	2.05	1.98
$100	1.36	1.31

Graph for Problem 40

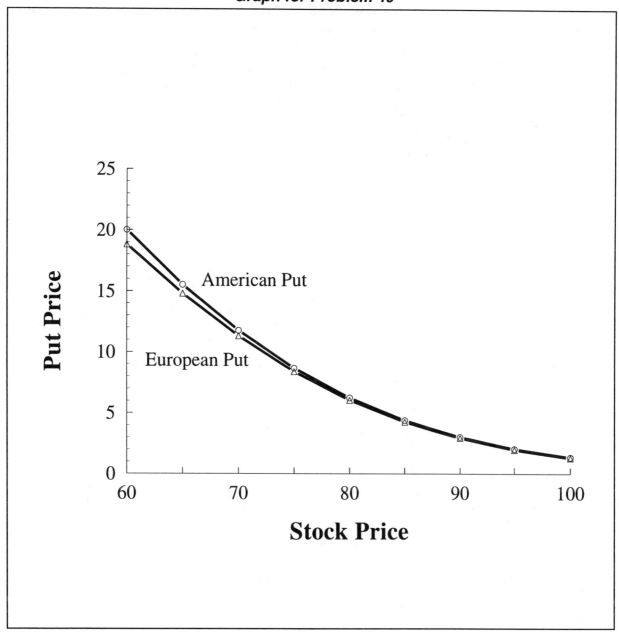

41. A stock has a current price of $80 and a standard deviation of .3. The risk–free rate is 7 percent. An American and a European call on this stock both expire in 200 days, and both have an exercise price of $70. The stock pays a continuous dividend of 3 percent. Find the price of the American call according to the analytic approximation formula, and find the price of the European option according to the Merton model. Complete the following table for the two options using the two respective models. How can you explain the price differentials reported in the table?

According to both the Merton model and the analytic approximation, the price is $13.63. The critical price for the call is $191.02.

Stock Price	American Call According to the Analytic Approximation	European Call According to the Merton Model
$60	2.37	2.37
$65	4.25	4.25
$70	6.80	6.80
$75	9.96	9.96
$80	13.63	13.63
$85	17.71	17.70
$90	22.07	22.07
$95	26.64	26.63
$100	31.34	31.33

The critical price for the call is $191.02. The option prices are virtually identical as the stock price is so far from the critical price and the early exercise feature has virtually no value. Only for stock prices above $90 does a difference in option values begin to emerge.

42. A stock has a current price of $80 and a standard deviation of .3. The risk–free rate is 7 percent. An American and a European call on this stock both expire in 200 days, and both have an exercise price of $70. If the stock is to pay a dividend it will be at a continuous rate, but the rate is uncertain. Alternative dividend rates are given in the table below. Find the price of the American call according to the analytic approximation formula, and find the price of the European option according to the Merton model for each dividend rate in the table. What do the price differentials in the table indicate about the importance of dividends for call pricing? For any of these dividend rates, should the American option be exercised now? If so, for which dividend rates?

The prices in the table show that the dividend becomes important as it becomes larger. At very low dividend rates, there is no difference, but a difference starts to emerge at the higher dividend rates. As the price of the American call always exceeds its intrinsic value, it should not be exercised. In fact, the critical value with $\delta = .05$ is $120.01, so the stock price is very far below that critical value.

Dividend Rate	American Call According to the Analytic Approximation	European Call According to the Merton Model
0.001	14.64	14.64
0.005	14.50	14.50
0.01	14.32	14.32
0.02	13.98	13.98
0.03	13.63	13.63
0.04	13.30	13.29
0.05	13.00	12.96

43. A stock sells for $110 and has a standard deviation of .2. The risk–free rate is 7 percent. An American put on this stock has an exercise price of $120 and expires in 200 days. Using the binomial model for an American put and a European put, complete the following table. Should the American put be exercised now? Explain.

Number of Periods	American Put Price	European Put Price
1	10.00	9.81
2	11.27	10.30
5	11.08	9.66
10	10.97	9.63
25	11.01	9.68
50	11.03	9.73
100	11.03	9.74
200	11.03	9.75

The American put should be exercised only if its price equals its intrinsic value. This occurs only for a single period model. For all other periods, the put price exceeds the intrinsic value. As the prices from the multi–period model are more reliable, the true price of the put is $11.03, and the put should not be exercised.

44. A stock sells for $110 and has a standard deviation of .2. The risk–free rate is 7 percent. An American put on this stock has an exercise price of $120 and expires in 200 days. Using the binomial model with 100 periods for an American put and a European put, complete the following table. From the table alone, what can you say about the correct exercise policy for the American put? Using the binomial model with 100 periods, find the exact stock price below which the American put should be exercised. Explain.

Stock Price	American Put Price	European Put Price
$90	30.00	25.77
$95	25.00	21.15
$100	20.00	16.87
$105	15.10	13.05
$110	11.30	9.74
$115	7.83	7.06
$120	5.38	4.90
$125	3.61	3.34
$130	2.34	2.19

From the table alone, we can say that the put should be exercised at a stock price of $100 or lower and that it should not be exercised at a stock price of $105 or higher. For stock prices of $100 or lower, the put price equals its intrinsic value, but for stock prices of $105 or higher, the put price exceeds its intrinsic value. By trial and error, it is possible to verify that the critical price, below which the put should be exercised, is $103.36. This is close to the analytical approximation critical price of $103.45.

45. The HOT100 stock index stands at 4000.00, and has a standard deviation of .20. The continuous dividend rate on the HOT100 is 3 percent, and the risk–free rate of interest is 5 percent. Using the Merton model, find the prices for the calls and puts shown in the table below.

Index Value	Call $X = 4000.0$ $T - t = 180$ days	Call $X = 3750.0$ $T - t = 90$ days	Put $X = 4000.0$ $T - t = 180$ days	Put $X = 3750.0$ $T - t = 90$ days
3500.0	53.54	55.77	507.52	285.62
3750.0	124.73	156.39	332.38	138.08
4000.0	239.45	320.89	200.77	54.42
4250.0	396.85	532.11	111.84	17.48
4500.0	588.98	767.42	57.64	4.63

46. The HOT100 stock index stands at 4000.00, and has a standard deviation of .20. The continuous dividend rate on the HOT100 is 3 percent, and the risk–free rate of interest is 5 percent. Using the Merton model, complete the table below for a call option with 180 days until expiration and an exercise price of $4000.0.

Index Value	DELTA	THETA	VEGA	RHO	GAMMA
4500.0	.8239	−200.6818	769.1956	1,538.0251	.0004
4250.0	.7059	−242.1371	996.0760	1,283.6826	.0006
4000.0	.5477	−253.5453	1,093.3300	962.2793	.0007
3750.0	.3693	−220.9529	983.7842	621.5020	.0007
3500.0	.2058	−152.8179	695.7750	328.8437	.0006

47. The HOT100 stock index stands at 4000.00, and has a standard deviation of .20. The continuous dividend rate on the HOT100 is 3 percent, and the risk–free rate of interest is 5 percent. Using the Merton model, complete the table below for a put option with 180 days until expiration and an exercise price of $4000.0.

Index Value	DELTA	THETA	VEGA	RHO	GAMMA
4500.0	−.1694	−138.5704	769.1956	−386.5329	.0004
4250.0	−.2795	−172.6359	996.0760	−640.8754	.0006
4000.0	−.4376	−176.6542	1,093.3300	−962.2793	.0007
3750.0	−.6160	−136.6720	983.7842	−1,303.0560	.0007
3500.0	−.7795	−61.1472	695.7750	−1,595.7143	.0006

48. The current dollar value of a German mark is $.6100, and the standard deviation of the mark is .25. The U.S. risk–free rate is 8 percent, while the German rate is 5 percent. European call and put options on the mark have an exercise price of $.6000 and expire in 250 days. What are these options worth today? If the German interest rate falls from 5 to 4 percent, what happens to the value of the options? Explain.

With δ = .05 the call is worth $.0592, and the put is worth $.0377. With δ = .04, the call is worth $.0617, and the put is worth $.0362. In effect, the foreign interest rate is like a dividend on a stock; it represents a leakage of value from the currency. Therefore, a lower dividend should raise the price of a call and diminish the price of a put. That is what happens in this example.

49. The current dollar value of a German mark is $.6100, and the standard deviation of the mark is .25. The U.S. risk–free rate is 8 percent, while the German rate is 5 percent. Consider an American and a European call on the mark with an exercise price of $.6000 that expires in 250 days. What are these options worth today? Should the American option be exercised now? If the German interest rate falls from 5 to 4 percent, what happens to the value of the options? Does it change the exercise decision? Explain.

With δ = .05, the European call is worth $.0592, and the American call is worth $.0593. With δ = .04, the European call is worth $.0617, and the American call is worth $.0617. In this example, the American call price always exceeds its intrinsic value, so it should not be exercised with either foreign interest rate.

50. Options now trade on the well–known widget futures contract. The current widget price is $100.0 per widget, and the futures price is $107.50. The futures contract expires in two years. The widget market is well–known for its strict adherence to cost–of–carry principles. The standard deviation of the futures price is .25. A European and an American call option on this futures have an exercise price of $105.00. What are the two options worth according to the Merton model and the analytic approximation for the American option? What would an American and European put be worth, assuming they have the same contract terms?

The interest rate is .0362, because $100e^{.0362(2)} = \$107.50$, as the cost–of–carry model would imply. Therefore, the Merton call price is $15.06, and the American analytic call price is $15.43. The Merton put price is $12.74, and the American analytic put price is $13.04.

51. The text has assumed that the cost–of–carry equals the risk–free rate. Explain how OPTION! could be used to value a futures option if the cost–of–carry were less than or greater than the risk–free rate.

The module for futures option pricing requires that the interest rate and the cost–of–carry be identical. However, OPTION! could be used to price a futures option in this situation by using either the stock index or foreign currency modules, which allow differential rates. In the case of the stock index module, the dividend yield plays the role of the cost–of–carry, while the foreign interest rate acts as the cost–of–carry in the foreign currency option pricing model.

52. Using OPTION! complete the following table for forward-start call and put options. S = 80; X = 75; T - t = 350 days; $\sigma = 0.4$; r = 0.08; and $\delta = 0.03$. As the table indicates, the day of the grant, tg, varies. Taking the call as an example, what do the values in the table indicate about how the option price varies with tg?

tg in Days	Forward-Start Call	Forward-Start Put
50	14.9620	7.1697
100	13.8203	6.5087
150	12.5754	5.7478
200	11.1892	4.8489
250	9.5904	3.7407
300	7.6105	2.2549
349	4.8686	0.0004

As tg increases, the option has very little life after it is granted. Thus, the value of the underlying option approaches its intrinsic value, discounted to the present. The underlying call with the given parameters and one day until expiration is worth 5.0103, very close to its intrinsic value. If that option is not to be obtained for 349 days, the value of the forward start option is 5.0103 discounted at the dividend rate of 0.03, which is 4.8686.

53. Complete the following table for the compound options shown below. Common parameters are: $S = 100$; $\sigma = 0.3$; $r = 0.01$; $\delta = 0.04$; $X = 100$; te = 100 days; and $T - t = 365$ days. As the table indicates, the exercise price of the compound option varies.

Exercise Price of Compound Option	Call-on-Call	Call-on-Put	Put-on-Call	Put-on-Put
5	9.5718	4.2820	0.2967	0.6020
10	6.0915	1.7936	1.6812	2.9786
15	3.7224	0.6395	4.1770	6.6894
20	2.2038	0.1908	7.5233	11.1055
25	1.2702	0.0460	11.4546	15.8255
30	0.7149	0.0085	15.7641	20.6529
35	0.3937	0.0011	20.3078	25.5104

54. Complete the following table for the compound options shown below. Common parameters are: S = 100; σ = 0.3; r = 0.01; δ = 0.04; X = 100; x = 10; and T - t = 365 days. As the table indicates, the expiration date of the compound option varies.

Expiration Date of Compound Option in days	Call-on-Call	Call-on-Put	Put-on-Call	Put-on-Put
50	5.1384	1.0598	0.8623	2.3790
100	6.0915	1.7936	1.6812	2.9786
150	6.9037	2.4053	2.3610	3.4579
200	7.6388	2.9611	2.9655	3.8831
250	8.3346	3.4936	3.5325	4.2868
300	9.0248	4.0304	4.0957	4.6966
350	9.7665	4.6168	4.7121	5.1577

55. Consider a European straddle with the following parameters: S = 50; X = 50; T- t = 365 days; σ = 0.5; r = 0.06; and δ = 0.03. What is the value of the straddle? Now consider a chooser option with the same parameters, but a varying choice date. Complete the table shown below. What does the table illustrate about the relationship between chooser prices and straddle prices?

Choice Date, tc, in Days	Chooser Value
0	10.1710
1	10.2493
50	13.0244
100	14.4635
150	15.5674
200	16.4954
250	17.3102
300	18.0441
350	18.7163
355	18.7807
360	18.8446
364	18.8953

The European call is worth 10.1710 and the European put is worth 8.7370, so the straddle is worth 18.9080. The table illustrates that the value of the chooser can range from the maximum price of either option in the straddle to the sum of the two options. If the choice must be made now, tc = 0, the chooser is worth 10.1710–just the value of the call. If the choice can be deferred until (almost) the expiration date, the chooser is worth 18.8953, just a hair under the value of the straddle itself.

56. Consider a European call and a European put with parameter values of: X = 70; T - t = 180 days; σ = 0.25; r = 0.1; and δ = 0.0. What is the value of the call and put if S = 80? Now consider a down-and-in call and a down-and-in put, with BARR = 80 and REBATE = 0.0. Using these data, complete the following table. What do these results suggest about the value of barrier options relative to plain vanilla options?

Stock Price	Down-and-In Call	Down-and-In Put
120	0.1379	0.0016
100	1.7885	0.0504
90	5.4142	0.2405
85	8.9605	0.4974
83	10.8597	0.6571
82	11.9322	0.7532
81	13.0943	0.8616
80.10	14.2218	0.9709
80.01	14.3390	0.9824

The European call is worth 14.3520, while the European put is worth 0.9837. The barrier options will be worth the same as the underlying options if they hit the barrier. Consider the call first. For prices well above the barrier, there is little chance of hitting the barrier, so the option has little value. However, if the price is right at the barrier, say 80.01, the down-and-in call is worth about the same as the European call. For the down-and-in put, there is little value for all the prices shown in the table, as the down-and-in put is still way out of the money even for the lowest price shown in the table. Thus, the call price is much more sensitive to the stock price that the put price for these values.

57. Consider an up-and-out call and an up-and-out put with the following common parameter values: T - t = 180 days; $\sigma = 0.2$; $r = 0.1$; $\delta = 0.03$; BARR = 100; and REBATE = 0. Complete the following table. What can you conclude from the completed table?

Stock Price	Up-and-Out Call X = 80	Up-and-Out Put X = 100
99	0.2733	0.6543
95	1.3940	3.4891
90	2.5741	7.4775
85	3.1139	11.8625
80	2.8546	16.5204
75	2.0297	21.3365
70	1.1034	26.2268

For a stock price near the barrier, say 99, both options are threatened with extinction, so each has little value. For stock prices below the barrier, the chance of extinction is less, so the value of the option will be more for that reason. However, we must also consider the likely payoffs. For the call, a low stock price reduces the chance of hitting the barrier, but it also implies little chance of a payoff. Thus, the call price is low for stock prices near the barrier and for stock prices below the exercise price. By contrast, the put fares very well for lower stock prices because a lower stock price reduces the risk of extinction from hitting the barrier and increases the payoff by being deeper in the money.

58. Consider an up-and-out call and an up-and-out put with the following common parameter values: $S = 98$; $\sigma = 0.2$; $r = 0.1$; $\delta = 0.03$; BARR = 100; and REBATE = 0. Complete the following table, and interpret the results.

T - t in Days	Up-and-Out Call X = 80	Up-and-Out Put X = 100
1	16.9140	1.9809
2	14.4919	1.9639
5	10.1013	1.9233
10	6.9951	1.8735
20	4.5085	1.8011
50	2.2054	1.6582
100	1.1105	1.5026
300	0.2778	1.1489

With one day until expiration, the call should be worth an amount near its intrinsic value of 20. However, the up-and-out call is worth considerably less because of the chance that the barrier will be hit and the option will be worthless. Notice that the longer the term to expiration, the lower the price of the call, reflecting the increased chance of hitting the barrier the longer the time until expiration. This chance is very high, because the stock price is right at the barrier now. The put is just in the money, so its value should be close to its intrinsic value. However, there is a chance of hitting the barrier in the next day, so its price is somewhat lower than the correlative European put. Further, for longer terms to expiration, the put's value decreases, and it does so for two reasons. First, a longer term to expiration reduces the present value of the payoff. Second, a longer term to expiration increases the chance that the option will hit the barrier.

59. A supershare is written with the following parameters: $S = 100$; $T - t = 365$ days; $\sigma = 0.4$; $r = 0.1$; and $\delta = 0.06$. Complete the following table for this supershare, assuming the varying upper and lower bounds in the table. What does the table illustrate about the influence of the bounds on the prices of supershares?

X_L	X_H	Supershare
70	80	0.1060
80	90	0.1072
90	100	0.0999
95	105	0.0943
100	110	0.0879
110	120	0.0741
120	130	0.0606

For every row in the table, the difference between the upper and lower bounds is the same. Only the location differs. The location affects the value of the supershare in two ways. First, the probability that the stock price will lie in these bands differs. With an initial stock price of 100, there is little chance that the terminal stock price will lie in the range of 70 to 80, for example. Second, the payoff on a supershare is a proportion of the portfolio's value that varies with the lower bound. So, the lower the bound, given that the supershare pays, the greater the value of the supershare.

60. Consider two lookback calls with the following common parameters: S = 100; T - t = 90 days; r = 0.06; and δ = 0.0. As the table indicates, the two calls are the same except one has MINPRI = 50, while the other has MINPRI = 95. Complete the following table and explain the differences in the prices of the two options.

Standard Deviation	Lookback Call MINPRI = 50	Lookback Call MINPRI = 95
0.1	50.7343	6.8623
0.2	50.7343	9.4658
0.3	50.7343	12.6941
0.4	50.7355	16.0141
0.5	50.7560	19.3036
0.6	50.8517	22.5234
0.9	52.1185	31.6506

The call with MINPRI = 50 is so deep-in-the-money, that the volatility of the stock has very little effect on the price. By contrast, the call with MINPRI = 95 is just barely in the money, so its price is very sensitive to the standard deviation.

61. Consider an option to exchange one asset for another with S_1 = 100; S_2 = 200; δ_1 = 0.01; δ_2 = 0.01; T - t = 90 days; and ρ = 0.0. Complete the following table and interpret your results.

$\sigma_1 = \sigma_2$	Price of Exchange Option
0.5	100.1990
0.4	99.8408
0.3	99.7576
0.2	99.7537
0.1	99.7537
0.05	99.7537

The option is deep-in-the-money. For lower risk levels on the two assets, there is little chance that anything will change. Therefore, as the risk is lowered, the value of the option converges to the present value of the difference in the price of the two assets, discounted at the dividend rate.

62. A call on the maximum of two assets has the following parameters: $S_1 = 100$; $S_2 = 100$; T - t = 365 days; $r = 0.08$; $\delta_1 = 0.0$; $\delta_2 = 0.0$; $\rho = 0.0$. Complete the following table and interpret your results.

$\sigma_1 = \sigma_2$	Call Price	Put Price
0.5	40.7129	5.3919
0.4	33.6835	3.7248
0.3	26.7364	2.2484
0.2	19.9409	1.0062
0.1	13.4736	0.1480
0.05	10.5122	0.0035
0.01	8.2526	0.0000
0.001	7.7448	0.0000
0.0001	7.6940	0.0000

The owner of the call only needs one asset to rise in price, so the greater the volatility the better. If there is no volatility, then the call owner must expect to receive the asset worth 100 upon payment of the exercise price in one year. Thus, the value of the call becomes essentially the difference between the price of the asset and the present value of the exercise price, which is 7.68837. The value of the call with $\sigma = 0.0001$ is very close to that. The owner of the put must surrender the more valuable asset for the exercise price. If there is very little risk, the asset prices are unlikely to change, so the option will most likely expire worthless. If there is considerable risk, there is a good chance that one of the assets will have a price drop to bring the put into the money.